THE

PARALYSIS OF MAINSTREAM

PROTESTANT LEADERSHIP

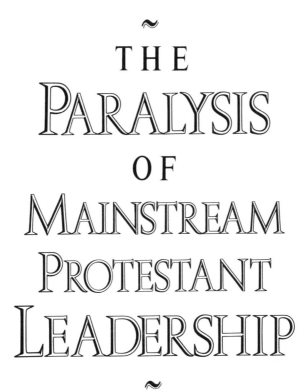

THE
PARALYSIS
OF
MAINSTREAM
PROTESTANT
LEADERSHIP

J. EDWARD
CAROTHERS

ABINGDON PRESS/NASHVILLE

THE PARALYSIS OF MAINSTREAM PROTESTANT LEADERSHIP

This book is printed on acid-free paper.

Carothers, J. Edward.
    The paralysis of mainstream Protestant leadership / J. Edward Carothers.
        p.   cm.
    Includes bibliographical references.
    ISBN 0-687-30072-X (alk. paper)
    1. Protestant churches—United States—History—20th century. 2. Leadership—Religious aspects—Christianity. 3. Church renewal-United States. 4. United States—Church history—20th century.
    I. Title.
    BR526.C39   1990
    280'.4'09730904—dc20   90-37336
                                                                CIP

ISBN 0-687-30072-X

"For the Time Being: A Christmas Oratorio" by W. H. Auden, on page 29, copyright 1944 and renewed 1972 by W. H. Auden. Reprinted from *W. H. Auden: Collected Poems* edited by Edward Mendelson by permission of Random House, Inc.

MANUFACTURED IN THE UNITED STATES OF AMERICA

CONTENTS

INTRODUCTION

This book is an insider's view of the mainstream Protestant problem of declining numbers and diminished influence. Any interpretation by any insider is bound to be suspect. Either it is prejudiced in the direction of praising too much or condemning too harshly. I try to avoid too much praising and condemning in order to favor a sympathetic but careful diagnosis of the church I admire and love.

In a real sense, every theology is a biography of the theologian. In some sense, a book of this kind exposes the writer. On September 15, 1930 I was accepted into the Methodist ministry. I served as a parish pastor for thirty-four years, a board executive for seven years, an adjunct faculty member of a theological school for five years, and a consultant on missiology for eight years. Were I to be granted another life on this earth I would choose to be a pastor of a parish. Throughout all of these years I have been deeply involved in ecumenical and interfaith work.

The decline in membership and influence of our mainstream Protestant churches is, for me, a heavy burden. I feel obligated to offer a diagnosis that has not been offered by anyone else. Although I began to see what is wrong with mainstream Protestantism fifty years ago, it was not until about twenty-five years ago that I began to feel certain that I was right in my understanding of the central problem.

My burden is very personal, but I have some obligation to

expose it clearly. It is the burden of knowing that the experience of epiphany—a completely encompassing awareness of the presence of God in an ordinary occasion—is too rarely known in mainstream Protestantism. In the last chapter of this book I describe our hunger for epiphany, and in a definite sense the entire thrust of what I write here is in the direction of enabling us to achieve that experience for which we hunger both night and day. Some may choose to read the last chapter first, but it should also be read last because I think that we cannot come to epiphany without encountering certain preliminary matters.

Although mainstream Protestantism has been losing members for nearly forty years and pastors and other church leaders are often puzzled and dismayed, this period of very painful discipline is necessary for all of us. It is almost axiomatic in human affairs that we do not make big changes in the way we live unless we are brought face to face with either great pain or the threat of death.

I do not think that mainstream Protestants are now facing death or anything like death. What I dread as a possibility is a stagnated mainstream Protestant movement that becomes a dragged-out case of continuing care—spoon-fed and kept quiet by tranquilizing tid-bits of superstition disguised as religious faith.

My reasons for this fear are fully explained in what follows, but I think I should confess that I find no substantial pleasure in offering the diagnosis. For one thing, I have been around for quite a while and I sometimes wonder if I should have given a greater energy to correcting what I then considered and continue to think of as flaws. Then I rationalize my guilt by saying to myself that I would have been totally unable to do what now I wish might have been done. There is at least one valuable element issuing from this looking backward: I am able to identify myself with what is wrong with our leadership, and that is where our problem must find its solution.

I believe that our leaders are organized into a number of castes. This must not be taken as a harsh judgment of our mainstream Protestant arrangement into tiers of order. We have achieved a distinctive organizational efficiency which allows for enormous freedom of thought and action. For more than two centuries we have been able to manage our affairs and do our work with volunteer workers carrying the heaviest load. The leadership caste doing the work in local churches is basic to our life.

It is also true that movement in mainstream Protestant churches is usually most effective when the initiatives come from the top caste: the bishops and their equivalents in denominations that do not like the idea of having such titles affixed to their chief executives. Very close to these officials are the bureaucrats or board executives who have real power because they manage large projects or programs and denominational funds. These two top castes are the real movers and shakers.

Getting the castes in our leadership system into tandem motion is not as difficult as one might suppose. Some remarkable accomplishments have been chalked up over the years to the credit of all the leaders and the rank and file who succeeded in achieving concerted group emphasis.

There is another group of mainstream Protestants that seems to be an independent order most of the time. These important leaders have their own caste system. I refer to our theological school faculties—and we have in America the finest theological schools in the world, at the present time. My proposal that they be brought into the solution of our problem will possibly be thought of as too difficult from the standpoint of scheduling and finance.

My reply to this very reasonable objection is that we have too much to gain to let the opportunity go without trying our best to make it happen. I feel convinced that our church leaders will benefit greatly, but they may not benefit more than our theological faculties, who will be thankful to know how well many church leaders have kept up with their studies and how capable these church leaders are when they go to work with a generous portion of new thoughts about God, the Bible, our world, and the human enterprise.

This book is dedicated to the leadership of all Christian churches, lay and clergy alike.

CHAPTER
I

THE MAINSTREAM PROTESTANTS
AT BAY

Approximately 80 million Protestants live in America. Of this number, about 40 million are mainstream church members, age thirteen and older. By *mainstream* I mean those Protestant denominations affiliated with the National Council of Churches of Christ. The Roman Catholic church has about 53 million members, including infants. About 40 percent of the American people have no religious affiliation of any kind.[1]

The average mainstream church member is close to fifty years of age. Mainstream churches are historically in the midstream of American culture. Their membership and influence has been declining for nearly forty years. The cause and cure of that decline is the burden of this book.

Our mainstream churches are not merely in decline; we who have been assigned responsibility to be leaders are frightened. We are huddled in dismay. We have a paralysis of mind and heart. We are dedicated to our tasks, but we have found that nothing we urge our people to do is curbing the stubborn decline of our membership, our ministry, and our cultural influence.

In this book I argue that we are declining because we, the clergy and lay leadership of mainstream Protestant churches, have failed to bring the new understandings of the Bible and theology being developed in our theological schools into interaction with the beliefs and actions of our church members. As a result, we have failed to allow for the fulfilling experience of the immanence of God—that is, epiphany—and to sustain an

11

ethic that includes all of God's creation. Our members are left with fundamentalist views of God and the Bible, scientistic notions of truth, and materialist approaches to life, whereas we who are leaders feel paralyzed and unable to pass on the new understandings that would revitalize our churches and ourselves.

Three cultural forces threaten the church by filling the vacuum left by our paralyzed leadership. I will briefly mention these forces here and describe them more fully later in this chapter.

1. **Fundamentalism:** a theological world view that is largely based on a literal interpretation of the Bible. G. M. Marsden's careful analysis of fundamentalism in American culture is basic to my understanding of it.[2] Marsden believes that American fundamentalism is almost always rooted in a literal interpretation of the Bible. This form of fundamentalism consistently develops a characteristic theology I will note later. Although Donald C. McKim sees at least ten forms of theology claiming a biblical basis in his book *What Christians Believe About the Bible* (1988), I confine my definition of fundamentalism to the form that employs a literal interpretation of the Bible. I suggest Carl F. H. Henry as a model for this type of fundamentalism.

2. **Scientism:** defined variously, but I am using it to describe our tendency to classify all truth in the limited terms defined by the inductive (scientific) method. This narrows human experience too much. It puts too much emphasis on limited rationalism and tends to be suspicious of poetic insights gained by metaphorical stretching of the mind and heart. It is suspicious of religion.

3. **Materialism:** the definition of material success as the primary value in life. We mainstream Protestants condemn materialism in social creeds which anger our members. Our church members cannot relate these social pronouncements to the religion that we proclaim. Of the three forces we have spawned to hold us at bay, our greedy materialism may be the most formidable to deal with.

Although mainstream Protestantism has helped to spawn these powerful cultural movements in America, we mainstream leaders show no signs of recognizing that this is so. We have not recognized the powerful forces threatening our church's life because many of us have been involved at some time or other in working hard to generate or perpetuate one or more of them. Many of us do not seem to know that we still sound like fundamentalists even though we are not. We sound like extreme rationalists, whether we are or not. The America that we mainstream Protestants have done so much to nurture is the greediest nation on earth if we measure our generosity by comparing it to our great wealth. Sweden gives about forty times as much as America does to the needs of the world if we measure Sweden's generosity by her total national wealth.

As different as these threatening forces are, they are united in powerful cacophony. Our contemporary mainstream churches often seem almost out of place in America. Our preaching and teaching of the Christian religion lacks mass appeal. Loud fundamentalistic theology, rampant scientific pronouncements, and the glitter of wealth are proving much more attractive. We who have been assigned leadership roles in our mainstream churches know that we cannot go back. But we seem to be afraid to go forward and run the great risks that forward movement demands.

We must understand the forces holding us at bay. We must move forward into a new era of mainstream Protestant ministry. We must become effective in a new world where people are forming new patterns of thought and new structures of social relationships. I argue that we will continue to decline in number and influence until we respond directly, openly, and aggressively to the cultural forces we have helped to spawn which now hold us at bay. Fundamentalism, scientism, and materialism arose together with mainstream Protestantism. We have a kinship with elements that confuse us and sap our powers.

The surprising complexity of this development is what confuses us to such serious extent. We are intellectually and spiritually paralyzed and cannot respond. We seem to think, or at least a great many of us do, that aggressive response to the forces that threaten our churches will also threaten our leadership status. We tend to think that we are in a no-win situation: if we do nothing, then we continue to be guardians of decline; if we act, then we imperil our security and status.

THE CHARACTER OF AMERICAN PROTESTANTISM

We should frequently review our mainstream Protestant history in America. Each denomination has certain distinguishing characteristics. It is useful for us to remember where we came from and why we mainstream Christians have churches with different shapes. We fall into serious error if we forget how valuable our differences have been to individuals, to the nation, and to the world.

Protestantism has its roots in Europe. However, it is fair to say that in America Protestantism came into full flower as an organized expression of Christianity which assigned real power to the laity. Even so, skillful clergy have often seized power and put the laity under some kind of authority exercised by the clergy. This tension between clergy and laity in mainstream Protestantism is fruitful because it assigns power to the laity while demanding leadership from the clergy. This has distinguished mainstream Protestantism with its two kinds of power: membership power and leadership power.

The mainstream denominations are situated in the center of the American cultural flow. They are the old, established churches with deep roots in the evolution of American culture. Their members come mainly from the middle and upper classes. The United Methodist Church is often called "the most American of the churches" because it was born with the American Revolution and its system of government closely parallels the pattern of the United States. It moved readily with the frontier because it had no regional loyalties based on the eastern seaboard. It appealed to the middle class. It was strong for personal piety, and it frowned on the display of wealth while it encouraged frugality. Methodists paid little attention to theology. The expanding nation was short on piety and bored with theology. The Methodist movement suited the mood, even if it did bankrupt theology at the expense of pious religion. The

United Methodists are still very American even though they have missionary outposts around the world and are increasingly ecumenical in spirit.

The Presbyterians would be ranked as "the most American" if one considered the amount of influence they exercised on the intellectual processes of the Founding Fathers. This stalwart mainstream denomination was solidly based in Princeton. It also had strong ties to the great intellectual giants of Europe and Britain. David Hume of Edinburgh was known as an atheist, but in spite of that his views were a topic of conversation among leading Presbyterians in Princeton in 1776. Although David Hume wasn't exactly a model for Presbyterians inside the church, the fact that he was of interest to many church leaders speaks eloquently of their intellectual vitality.

Another notable European who had great influence on the Presbyterians of Princeton was Adam Smith, whose *The Wealth of Nations* was published in 1776. The intellectual Presbyterians in Princeton knew very well that Smith's earlier work, *The Theory of Moral Sentiments,* was intended by Smith as an introduction to his *Wealth of Nations.* In his first book, Smith said that human beings are generous and compassionate by nature. His second book assumed that in a social order with free competition the self-interest of the successful will inevitably turn their natural generosity and compassion toward the needs of the less successful. This trickle down theory has been proved false in American life, but Smith's cheery thesis still seems to prevail. Adam Smith's views were revived with renewed vitality during the Carter and Reagan administrations.

In New England the Congregational Church provided an impressive quality of intellectual and spiritual leadership. Today the Congregational Church is gathered into the United Church of Christ, which has settled down into a complacent relationship with an American culture it periodically criticizes with sharp tongue. But the United Church of Christ retains its traditional interest in achieving a successful economic status and a stately social dignity.

The Germans, Bavarians, and Scandinavians brought their forms of Lutheran tradition and planted them wherever they settled. There has been a tenacity or durability in their faith. The Baptists were born in Rhode Island and have been stout defenders of a church separated from the state. The Reformed Church held a leading role in Albany and the Hudson Valley, although it has not grown much in number.

Taken as a whole, these mainstream Christian Protestants had much in common. Although they divided on Sundays for separate services of worship and each pulpit had its own traditional language and images, these mainstreamers worked well together during the week. They had in common a love of their freedom from authoritative controls, a dedication to earning money and to economic independence, and a wide-open curiosity to know everything they could learn about the new world.

It was in these old mainstream Protestant churches that American culture found its spiritual energy to endure painful hardships while praying for a better world. It is also in these churches that American culture found support for three forces that now threaten and puzzle mainstream Protestants: fundamentalism, scientism, and materialism.

FUNDAMENTALISM

Fundamentalism of one kind or another thrives in times of intellectual and cultural turmoil. Christian fundamentalism in America has surged into new levels of energy at the same time that Jewish fundamentalism in Israel and Muslim fundamentalism in Iran have taken on new life. American Protestant fundamentalism is not a solid block of like-minded Christians. G. M. Marsden has traced the ways that fundamentalists differ from one another.[3] I want to avoid leaving the impression that I am holding fundamentalists in contempt or speaking about them in derisive tone. That I think they are generally wrong in many of their positions will become very clear, but I wish to make it equally clear that there are reasons why fundamentalist Protestantism has become more aggressive and self-confident.

By *fundamentalism* I mean biblical literalism and the theological views that usually attend such literalism. Understanding the Bible as God's inerrant word is the most conservative of all literalistic positions. All data in the Bible enjoys equal status of factuality. Whatever the Bible says is true and final. This doctrine of the inerrancy of the Bible is preceded by a doctrine of inspiration that has many versions. Each of these variations reinforces the argument that the Bible is a carrier of true knowledge.

More moderate are relaxed fundamentalists who differ from one another mainly in the ways that they shade their interpretations. Some will say that the truth of God's voice comes through the noisy words of the Bible just as the singer's true voice comes through the noise of a phonograph record. We must learn how to hear the true voice in spite of the orchestra, surface noise, and equipment faults. This is Swiss theologian Emil Brunner's way of speaking about the Bible as the Word of God. I consider such a view to be biblical literalism and fundamentalism, although Brunner would deny being a fundamentalist.

Mainstream Protestants have had very little difficulty discarding biblical inerrancy, but have had real problems with biblical literalism. Whereas our better theological schools have long since gone far ahead of any form of biblical literalism, we mainstream leaders have either failed to keep up with our theological schools or have not been able to figure out ways to bring our members to a better understanding of the Bible and a corresponding advance in their theological perceptions. The Bible is central to mainstream Protestantism, yet mainstream Protestants have not reaped the benefits of biblical scholarship which goes beyond literalism to discover richer values.

A characteristic theology often grows out of biblical literalism. This theology has doctrines that include the Virgin Birth, belief in miracles, a belief in the supernatural nature of Jesus who is the Christ, the physical resurrection of dead bodies, the Second Coming of Jesus, and sometimes the special baptism of the Holy Spirit which causes a believer to speak in unknown tongues. The keystone of Protestant fundamentalism is its theology which predicts hell for unbelievers and promises heavenly reward for believers. Heaven and hell give theological fundamentalism a punishment-reward system. This notion of retribution seems to have very little effect on ethics (note the televangelist scandals), but it is a strong inducement to join the church and to support the church with money. Fundamentalist church growth can be explained in part by this emphasis on the soul's ultimate destiny.

Although strict fundamentalism is outside the mainstream Protestant churches for the most part, all of the mainstream denominations still harbor vestiges of fundamentalism. Most mainstream leaders advocate a very lukewarm fundamentalism and a watered-down biblical literalism. This generates a church characterized by an intellectual vagueness in theology and a confusing view of the Bible. We say that we are not fundamentalists but we sound like fundamentalists when we sing, pray, teach, and preach literal biblical doctrines such as the virgin birth or the physical resurrection of Jesus.

SCIENTISM

By *scientism* I mean the tendency to classify all truth in the limited terms of inductive (scientific) inquiry. This method of inquiry has given us a world of technological advances. The inductive method of gathering data before drawing conclusions has also taught us to question traditional beliefs about almost everything. Belief in the Bible as a complete storehouse of knowledge seems out of place in a world where new knowledge is supposed to be uncovered daily.

The unquestionable triumphs of the scientific revolution have combined to create a certain contempt for the past. People casually speak of the pre-scientific era as if it were a time of total darkness. It does not occur to many people that there may have been some remarkable perceptions of the true nature of things even before the time of Copernicus and those who followed him.

The scientific method has been the cause of nervous anxiety in the religious fraternity for more than a century. Don Cupitt of Emmanuel College, Cambridge, has traced this history in his British television series and in his book *The Sea of Faith*.[4] Cupitt argues that the erosion of traditional belief by the new knowledge flowing out of the scientific method has destroyed the framework of traditional faith. His analysis is accurately descriptive of what I see in American mainstream Protestantism.

American mainstream Protestants were early advocates of education leading to higher skills in science and industry. John Wesley's "Methodists" got their name from their commitment to a disciplined schedule of life which included trying to help people who suffered sickness and poverty. The Methodist classes included practical guidance in how to get out of poverty by learning the secrets of reading, writing, and managing a household to stay out of debtor's prison. It is not a long way from this kind of interest to a real commitment to higher education for everybody, and mainstream Protestants were committed to this goal from the start.

Higher education, in the era of new rationalism, inevitably resulted in a common belief that true and trustworthy ideas must have tangible proofs that can be tested. Factual truth must be proved with tangible evidence that can be measured or weighed in some way. The scientific method limits too narrowly the range of valid experiences of the universe. This method leaves little room for religious experience. We have been "educated away" from thinking of the religious life as a natural and valid way of entering into an experience of God in the ordinary things that happen as we work, play, worship, and love. The immediate immanence of God which is basic to the experience of epiphany is hard for us to grasp. Give me the evidence in hard data, we say to one another, or don't ask me to believe what you say.

The scientific definition of how human beings come to truth is useful in dealing with some aspects of our relationship to the world. We need scientific methods, but that does not mean that we have no other way of knowing something that is true about our lives in this vast universe where God moves in and beyond the crevices.

The scientific method has little or no use in my agony of coming to terms with the death of my beloved, or the unutterable ecstasy of knowing the beauty of the world in a lonely star on a winter's night. There are those realms of imagination through which we reach beyond what we can see, touch, smell, taste, feel, or measure. There is a spiritual side to human existence. The scientific method quite properly does not claim to deal with its fullest dimension.

We admire the scientific method because it protects us from being reckless with truth. All of us must remain alert to the mischief that is done in the name of spiritual living. Gurus and New Age prophets abound, and mainstream Protestants have learned to be wary. We do not rejoice when some fundamentalists make television appeals for huge sums of money on the grounds that they have had special revelations from God. We are cautious of reckless and boastful claims of special spiritual powers made by anyone.

Scientism arises when the scientific method is extended beyond its proper bounds. Scientism cuts out the overtones. It stays with the strict fact that middle C will vibrate only a certain number of times per second. Any musician knows the ugliness of a note without the overtones. We need to know all about middle C and its vibrations if we can, but we have great music only when we get the overtones. We need science, but we need more than science.

One of our real difficulties is in our religious literature. The experience of God is usually described in spectacular terms. This can mislead us into looking to science for the full understanding of ordinary experience. It has become almost impossible for us to think that telling the truth or giving a thirsty person a cup of pure, cold water can be a religious experience of God. We have become cold-minded rationalists, and poetry delights not our souls.

In the early nineteenth century, when pietism and high emotionalism were accepted as a source of religious truth, mainstream Protestants were founding their colleges and universities where people would be told that real truth comes from scientific research. Although dedicated to intellectual matters, these institutions of learning rode two horses. In scientific studies, one kept a cool head and subdued emotions. In religious experience, one drew deeply from emotional sources and subdued intellect. It is doubtful that anyone could have predicted that mainstream Protestants were educating them-selves to doubt the validity of religious experience in extraordinary terms. Nor could it have been known, until lately, that mainstream Protestants would find themselves incapable of the experience of epiphany—the completely encompassing awareness of the presence of God in an ordinary occasion.

Today the scientific method has caught the mainstream churches with an inadequate theology and a complete inability to nurture religious experience in terms of what the graduating students have come to know about their universe. How can one pray to ask God to change the rules of a natural order? What is there to worship in a universe born in a Bang only to end in another Bang? The world view emerging out of scientific inquiry and the experience of working as scientists has undermined our literal view of how we hold our relationship with God. We cannot be alive to the immediate immanence of God because we look for the wrong things in religious experience.

There is grim irony in the fact that the mainstream churches that are half-hearted in their theology and lukewarm about the religious experience of God can't minister to most of the graduates of their colleges and universities. These graduates may continue to hold a formal church membership and attend a few festival occasions, but the continued falling away of the highly educated Protestants is a solemn warning about the future. Even those Americans who have not had the benefits of higher education have been captured by the scientific view of a world where blind forces play with human destiny.

MATERIALISM

Materialism is the tendency to regard material success as the primary value of life. American Protestantism has provided the spiritual motivation for the gathering of material wealth and has been largely responsible for the emergence of a greedy nation. This is an indictment that has new documentation every day.[5]

Mainstream Protestants provided a needed spiritual em-phasis in the new nation being founded after the Revolution.

Whereas a few people had some wealth, most of the people were very poor. An emphasis on careful management of personal affairs was needed. Mainstream Protestantism offered spiritual encouragement for saving money and gathering wealth with hymns, prayers, sermons, and churchly admonitions of various kinds. There was no welfare system. Frugality and holiness went together, and it was not a bad combination in early America.

Encouragement to acquire and save wealth was a sustained emphasis in mainstream Protestantism which formed a cultural attitude in America. Calvin's influence on the Presbyterians led to a rugged individualistic conviction that God blesses those who carefully and tightly manage their assets. Luther's influence was earthy, and it favored economic goals. The rich natural resources of a vast continent were exactly right for the Protestant reformation to demonstrate its vitality of freedom from controls of either church or state. Rugged individualism required financial independence.

The nation expanded with a strong cultural conviction that anybody who really wanted to gain wealth could do it. In this new land of abundance, freedom to use your best talents to get the greatest wealth possible was justified by religion. Failure to achieve economic self-support was a sign of laziness, and laziness was a sin. Although mainstream Protestantism sometimes showed signs of appreciating relaxation, art, music, and recreation, there was always a lingering suspicion that too much of this sort of thing would soften one's ability to work hard and earn a good living.

Umberto Eco describes this religious sanctioning of material wealth like this: "In the United States, there's a Puritan ethic and a mythology of success. He who is successful is good. In Latin countries, in Catholic countries, a successful person is a sinner. In Puritan countries, success shows God's benevolence. In Catholic countries, you're sure God loves you only when you've suffered."[6]

The United States did not develop without great energy of spirit and will. The hard work posed by the expanding frontiers across the continent demanded physical labors we cannot fully appreciate. The risks that people had to run with disease, childbirth, heat, cold, rain, and frost were life threatening year round. It took great faith to do what Americans did in opening up a new continent, and mainstream Protestantism was a primary source of that faith.

Controls over personal behavior were necessary in developing North America, and mainstream Protestantism proclaimed how Divine Powers favored the industrious and sober individual who had enough faith to suffer hardship until God finally came through with rewards. These rewards were tangible proof of God's approval. The mainstream Protestants combined their emphasis on sobriety and hard work with promises of earthly blessings from God. Hard work and sobriety were essential, and the people supported these values even when they violated them. Legendary figures of violence, sin, and murder constitute the mythologies of the West and provide entertainment in television and in fiction, but bad guys always lose. The mainstream Protestant ethic always wins in romantic Western sagas.

On the holy virtues associated with the acquisition of goods, the saving of money, and the holiness of hard work to get what you got, the mainstream Protestants were united. At the same time, the mainstream Christians manifested a remarkable concern for doing good works. While they were busy creating a materialistic America, their reading of the Bible and the admonitions of their traditions gave them a conscience: they had genuine sympathy for people who were poor and in need of help. They gave substantial attention to works of charity. All over the nation they established hospitals, homes, schools, and works of mercy which have become permanent institutions. A few who became extremely wealthy gave large sums to build these monuments to their acquired wealth.

The fact that America developed as a nation given to charitable causes, largely sponsored by the churches, does not nullify the charge that at the same time the well-meaning mainstream Protestant Christians were nurturing a materialistic society that has become a global scandal. Not until the twentieth century was two decades old did anyone see that charity could not make economic justice a possibility for a substantial minority of Americans. When the so-called Social Gospel emerged, the mainstream Protestant leaders shrank back. It challenged their assumptions about the higher values of hard work and a quiet piety of prayer and faithful industry. To think that there was anything wrong with the American way of doing business was close to atheism, socialism, or some other awful heresy.

Economist Leonard Silk, who writes for *The New York Times,* describes poverty in the United States. The rich are getting richer and the poor are becoming poorer. From 1979 to 1986, the rich became richer by 13.8 percent. The poor became poorer by 10.9 percent. Silk says that the most disturbing thing of all is something sociologist Oscar Lewis pointed out almost a quarter of a century ago. America has developed a huge underclass which has grown relentlessly and is still growing today.[7]

This is a global scandal. America is a nation with a majority living in wealth and abundance. Its Christian churches are the wealthiest in the world, yet a substantial minority of Americans now suffer from gruesome poverty, medical neglect, malnutrition, slum dwellings, denial of education, and much more.

The American people are puzzled. They have a conscience about people in need. They are mystified when people in America fall behind the economic parade. Well-to-do Americans feel sorry for the people who cannot keep up, but they do not understand why all cannot be winners. After all, laziness is wicked, and anybody who works hard can be a winner. The mainstream Protestants, who did so much to create this spirit of misunderstanding, have a major responsibility to correct it.

Mainstream Protestants should not be puzzled by the dismaying spectacle of people mired in poverty. For many years we have had hard data on why the poor have such a terrible time getting out of poverty. If we are puzzled, then it is not because there is nothing to be known. The real reason we are puzzled is that we don't like to hear the truth. Namely, the poor are kept in their poverty by the attitudes of the middle and upper classes. The Protestant ethic of hard work and careful management has become the all-too-evident credo of self-interest and greed.

There are numerous systems within our economy, including

education, health care, communications, and the like. We cannot get along without them. Yet the data show that the poor are kept in poverty by the attitudes of prosperous Americans who favor our various systems as they stand because these systems serve to their advantage.[8]

Professor Benjamin DeMott, referring to Richard Hofstader, the historian, establishes this point: "Evangelical Protestantism induced a conception of responsibility according to which 'everyone was in some serious sense responsible for everything,' and self-deception entered because the typical person in whom the sense of guilt and shame was quickened had no intention of making any basic changes in a society in which he was so typically a prosperous and respectable figure."[9]

I believe it is true that the American people do not want to do what is necessary to rid the nation of an underclass trapped in poverty and great suffering. We want to be charitable and kind, but we are afraid that it would undermine our prosperity if changes were made in our systems so that the poor could have a decent chance.

THE SEPARATION OF THEOLOGY AND ETHIC

At the turn of the century, the conscience of mainstream Protestant churches was challenged in a new depth by the Social Gospel. The Western expansion had ended, and industrial America was in full swing. Walter Rauschenbusch, a Baptist preacher and teacher, articulated a challenge to the mainstream Protestants. On behalf of the poor he called for social reforms. Some of the mainstream denominations responded by making social pronouncements on matters of social justice.

These social pronouncements were eventually phrased into social creeds in one form or another. By the end of World War II, some of the mainstream denominations were challenging fundamental American practices that had become established parts of the social fabric. The rights of laboring people to organize and to seek a fair wage were advocated by church resolutions. These same churches had industrial managers who were hot in their opposition to such resolutions. Much to the mainstream Protestants' surprise, the laboring class was not well represented in their church memberships unless workers had achieved some prosperity. Also, the American work force was increasingly derived from the immigrant populations from Roman Catholic traditions in Europe. The labor movement soon became predominantly Roman Catholic.

The conscience of mainstream Protestants was working overtime, and their Social Gospel pointed toward the rescue of people who were not members of their churches, for the most part. The mainstream ranks had become prosperous, and their social ethic was challenging their consciences by calling attention to the plight of oppressed people who were not in their churches. This new ethic called for social change, and this was not what mainstream Protestants wanted to hear from their leadership. They did not want change because their favorable situation would probably be disturbed by any changes in social systems.

When the Taft-Hartley Act became the law of the nation in 1947, it supported collective bargaining. Prominent mainstream leaders had favored its adoption. Protestant industrial managers did not meekly fall into line. They shifted their opposition to a new battle front and concentrated on getting state laws restricting union activities. When 1950 finally rolled around, most of the mainstream church members were out of touch with the leadership levels that still advocated the Social Gospel. Their theology wasn't up to all this political maneuvering. They could not see what this had to do with Jesus, God, or their eternal destiny. The Social Gospel seemed a far cry from a life of prayer in the context of reflection. In what seems like total lack of awareness, strong mainstream clergy and other leaders continued to hammer away at a social ethic that the members could not link to their religion.

The mainstream Protestants had been taught to value their freedom, so whenever a church resolution appeared to infringe on their economic activities, it was unwelcome. Then why go to all the trouble of passing resolutions if the membership has no serious obligation to pay any attention to the resolutions?

Adopted resolutions that call for specific lines of action and behavior by the church members do not always seem to have any relationship to the Christian faith as it is understood by the people "back home" in the churches. Many studies document this.[10] Mainstream Protestant preaching and programs of adult education have not prepared the people in the pews with a theological basis for supporting the resolutions on social ethics that the denominations adopt. By far, most of these social ethics resolutions strike at mainstream Protestant greediness. In spite of good resolutions, our devoted church members have a basic theology that justifies their ownership of goods. Members are not about to part with their goods just because a resolution is adopted by their church.

This is a very serious matter. It is clear enough to many white Christians that black people are being denied their God-given rights to a dignified place in society. It was significant to notice in the 1950s and 1960s how much easier it was for white people to believe in racial equality when they lived in towns or neighborhoods that were strictly white. When a black family bought a house in one of these strictly white neighborhoods, it was not nearly so easy for some of the white people to agree with their mainstream Protestant church pronouncement about racial dignity and equality. Their religious faith didn't support their church's position.

Although Martin Luther King, Jr. gave a religious dimension to the civil rights movement at a time when it threatened to become civil strife, there was in the white community a notable lack of deep religious feeling that the Christian faith required a long-term commitment to help black people become free from new forms of slavery. The racial issue is only one illustration of the general predicament of the mainstream Protestant church which lacks a theology to sustain a social ethic defined by leadership.

By the time we mainstream Protestants had reached our peak in 1950, the signs of trouble were already being noticed by a few. When our membership began to decline in successive annual reports, all mainstream Protestant leaders began to take notice. Our response was typically bureaucratic. We called for a renewed emphasis on going out into the highways and byways to bring in new members and to restore the dropouts. Mass evangelism had worked before World War I, but its appeal had since declined.

PARALYSIS OF PROTESTANTISM

By the late 1980s, the paralysis now affecting mainstream Protestantism was in place. I use the metaphor of paralysis with care. The thinking powers of leaders—and the whole system of nerve connections and muscles of the mainstream denominations—seemed incapable of response to the factors threatening their bodies.

In 1966, Dean Kelley's excellent book, *Why the Conservative Churches Are Growing*[11], exerted real influence on mainstream leaders. Kelley argued that the conservative churches were growing because they demanded something of their members. In my view he correctly appraised the reason for the growth of conservative churches.

His analysis does not explain why the mainstream Protestant churches are declining. Many mainstream leaders who studied Kelley's superb book were baffled by his conclusion. How could they demand more of their members? They already knew they were in trouble for demanding too much by way of a social ethic calling for burdensome changes. These leaders were not stupid. They knew how hard they had been working to get their church members to support social changes. They knew that the church members didn't accept that demand. Instead of accepting the demand, members stayed home from church. They quit inviting new people to attend. Many quietly dropped out. All because they saw no connection between their religion and what they were being asked to take as their personal task in saving the world and their own souls. Kelley's excellent analysis of the conservative churches might fit those churches, but mainline leaders knew full well that it did not fit their churches.

Baffled by membership and financial decline, mainstream Protestant leadership is paralyzed by confusion and anxiety. We mainstream church leaders know that we are not leaders anymore because our members are in rebellion against the social ethic that we proclaim and that their theology and understanding of the Bible do not support. We know our membership can win the rebellion by cutting off funds or dropping their membership. We are paralyzed by what we know about our helplessness in the face of all this.

We know we cannot accept the fundamentalistic theology and Biblical literalism. The new knowledge about the Bible plus emerging theological perceptions are now our heavy burdens. We have gotten into trouble when we have tried to share with our church members some of the more recent developments in biblical and theological studies. We know we must go forward, but we fear what lies ahead for all of us. Aware of uncertainty, we are often devoid of hope. The more we explore the advancing frontiers of biblical and theological studies, the more diverse they seem to us. The size of our task frightens us. But "something" lures us onward, and we cannot turn back.

We are captured, as were the legendary Wise Men. We have seen the Star that calls all of us forward, but we dread to follow the Star because it means a new obedience to higher and more costly ethical demands.

With uncanny perception, W. H. Auden touched an essential element in the way God works in our world. In his Christmas Oratorio, *For the Time Being,* the Wise Men prepare to follow the Star to see where it may lead them. Then the Star speaks to them as it does to us:

> I am that star most dreaded by the wise,
> For they are drawn against their will to me,
> Yet read in my procession through the skies
> The doom of orthodox sophrosyne:
>
> ———————
>
> ———————
>
> Beware. All those who follow me are led
> Onto that Glassy Mountain where are no
> Footholds for logic, ————————————
> ——————————————————————.[12]

Sophrosyne is an uncommon word Auden uses to make his point. It means prudence, moderation, caution. We mainstream

Protestant leaders know that biblical scholarship has advanced beyond our competent use and is no longer being reflected in our educational programs and our preaching. We know that a psychologized religion has produced a purely secularized membership that is increasingly unable to pray, worship, or act in obedience to God. We know from experience how greed has infected all of us in the household of faith.

We have dreaded following the Star for these past two generations. We have dreaded it so much that we have found a way to avoid "that Glassy Mountain where are no footholds for logic."[13] We have found our escape from the authentic voice of Jesus by psychologizing religion. It worked fairly well for us until of late. Let us now step forward and see how we have been escaping from our real function as pastors, teachers, and leaders who are responsible for the ministries of vital Christian faith which gives a true sense of meaning, sustains a whole ecological ethic, and also evokes the experience of epiphany.

C H A P T E R
II

PSYCHOLOGIZING RELIGION

When our theology gradually lost its hold on our minds and hearts and our understanding of the Bible was invaded by new scholarship that we could hardly assimilate, we who were charged with mainstream leadership roles found our refuge in psychology. Our members were ready to go with us for two major reasons.

First, we needed all the help we could get to remain mentally healthy in a society that was increasingly complex. The twentieth century brought new forms of stress with its burgeoning technology made possible by scientific discoveries. Radical shifts were taking place in such matters as sexual behavior, birth control, population expansion, and environmental dangers. Underneath the need for help in making better adjustment to life was an unspoken anxiety that our solitary lives may not be so important to God after all. Psychology was an escape from the main question, at least in this regard, because it called for us to concentrate on being well adjusted in a world we could not change or understand. It was also a lot easier to adjust our responses than it was to advance into a new theology that called us into a new ethic based on the sacredness and interdependence of all creation.

Second, a new theology that asked us to be more responsible to life was too demanding. Psychology was an attractive substitute for religion because it enabled us to evade a whole ecological ethic that called for us to change our ways of doing business. We knew that our church members had great difficulty in relating prophetic preaching and teaching to their beliefs about God, Jesus, prayer, and the meaning of life. Yet our traditional theology had thrown us into the social arena because we had inherited from Jesus and our tradition a strong social sensitivity we could not ignore. Out of this tradition the Social Gospel had sprung, but our theology did not sustain it. Our members concluded that "social action" leaders were subversive radicals. Increasingly, the members in the main-stream Protestant churches found more pleasure and satisfaction in trying to find suitable adjustments to life rather than in trying to change social conditions for others. Psychology was given a religious dress and we turned to it in great relief. Few escaped the charms of psychic stroking of our little neurotic streaks.

With these two very good reasons for doing so, we adopted psychology and used it as a substitute for religion. We borrowed from Freud, Adler, Jung, and all their disciples. We carefully adorned psychology with Scripture and theological terms. This was not difficult to do because the Bible and Christian theology are both historically devoted to a serious study of human motives and adaptations in living. Christianity is basically committed to the cure of souls, and we were hardly aware that we were confining the Gospel to the narrow focus of becoming nicely adjusted in a twisted world.

We were skating on thin ice. Beneath our surface consciousness a very deep ocean of spiritual hunger and intellectual despair was developing in our lives. Perhaps we sensed this all along, for we gave ourselves with great dedication to making a psychologized religion serve the deepest needs of human life confronting a strange world. For a half century we thought we were succeeding.

At one stage, after graduating from theological school, my situation was very favorable for advanced work, and I threw my energies into becoming qualified as a consulting psychologist under the prevailing standards. I am convinced that my pastoral work was made much more effective, and I am in favor of a pastoral ministry that is competently trained in psychology, but it took me too long to realize that psychologized Christianity is not the full answer to our deepest needs. I discovered, as so many others have, that it is much easier to proclaim a psychologized religion. It is much harder work to incorporate new biblical and theological developments into both preaching and teaching; the chief difficulty being the tentative nature of many of the most recent and interesting developments. Most of us have not learned how to keep people in touch with growing edges of knowledge when there is often very little consensus on important points.

We have yet to discover how faith is nurtured by bold candor in honoring valid doubts or in suspending opinion. Failing to speak clearly in new theological terms and neglecting biblical scholarship, we have suffered an invisible but deadly erosion of the faith that was once considered to be established on everlasting foundations. We suffer because a rigid theology will not stand up to the new facts of the unfolding social developments and new knowledge about the wonders of the universe. We have been busily psychologizing religion at the very time we should have been innovative in theology and dynamic in spreading new biblical scholarship. We should have long ago invited our entire church membership into the open arena where biblical and theological questions do not have final answers.

All of us got something good out of the psychologized form of the Christian religion. No doubt many of us have been helped over rough spots by it. Indeed, psychologized Christianity was good enough to pass for real religion for a long time. But there was a flaw that we did not see because we lacked the experience to see it. Psychologized Christianity lacks depth. It does not and cannot deal adequately with the problem of meaning. It cannot offer a satisfying answer to the ultimate cry of each human soul: "What does my life mean in this Vastness?"

How were we taken in by the promises of psychologized religion? When the influences of such pioneers as Freud, Adler, and Jung caused a proliferation of psychological schools in America, each of the various schools followed their leaders by mixing them together in various ways. But regardless of how this school of thought or that one may have differed in small ways, one common interest emerged in all forms of psychologized religion: the goal of life is to be well adjusted to circumstances. Psychologized religion turns life in upon itself.

One cannot find fault with a serious effort to help people find ways of discovering resources for living in a world where science-based technology so often upsets familiar patterns of existence. The advent of psychology was a kind of narrowing into specific focus the insights of ancient religions, mythologies, legends, and theologies. That it came out as a discipline of the mind and emotion was only superficially apparent. But there was a deceptive element in the psychologizing of our faith.

As Don Browning has shown, we plastered over our psychologized religion a thin layer of theology. We hinted here and there at the meaning of human life. These thin veneers of theology failed to meet the need, but the mere fact that we tacked them into our pastoral work and preaching shows us how we are inevitably drawn into making assumptions or announcements about the ultimate meaning of human existence. Browning argues that when psychologists do this they are creating a pseudo-theology.[1] He does not disparage the psychologists; he only shows us how easily we may confuse ourselves into thinking that we are being theologians when we are actually examining human nature.

THE RISE OF PSYCHOLOGY

It is probably impossible to say exactly when a turn in the tides of opinion takes place, but in the opening years of this century psychology began to come of age in America. Personality treatments were expanding into a thriving industry that promised healing for the human soul. While the headlines debated the significance of Freud, Adler, and Jung of Europe, there were also truly great students of human behavior in America. Harry Stack Sullivan was a great teacher who wrote little, but his skill in the psychiatric interview was widely proclaimed. He became an early model for pastors who were trying to learn how to listen and not to do all of the talking.

Flanders Dunbar's *Emotions and Bodily Changes* was first printed in 1935 and was regularly revised until 1955. Its first bibliography listed nearly 1,800 books and articles on the subject of how emotions are linked to bodily functions, and vice versa. Drug therapy was soon to emerge. This launched an interest in psychosomatic medicine which has become firmly established. These developments bordered on traditional pastoral care of the flock. If a suffering person could not find help in a pill, then we who were highly trained in psychosomatics would approach the body through the mind. Hardly anyone seemed to be aware of the subtle insinuation that the soul (psyche/mind/spirit) was only a means allowing us to help heal the body. It was therefore reasonable to turn to chemicals if we could, because that was an easier and faster cure. Religious faith played second fiddle to drugs. Pastors who cared deeply about improving their skills took clinical training in hospitals and learned to distance themselves from suffering people who were mainly under the care of physicians. We were aware that most of the sick suffered from psychogenic ailments, but even the most competent of these pastors tended to overlook the theological roots of much human suffering.

The mainstream Protestants were out in front on this movement, and it shows a deep concern for the kind of suffering Americans had known so intimately during and after the Great Depression of the 1930s. By the 1950s our theological schools had developed significant emphasis on better training in pastoral care. These courses were taught by competent scholars who often brought into their courses recognized guest scholars from nearby psychiatric institutions. This training was in harmony with the church's historic concern for the healing of souls. Historian John T. McNeil became the chief custodian of this great tradition.

McNeil's book *The History of the Cure of Souls* could not have documented the serious side-effect of the psychologization movement because he retired about the time that this phenomenon had advanced to be a real obstacle in mainstream Protestantism. From his historical study, however, we can see how the American emphasis on making happy adjustments to life bonded with the American love of wealth. Mainstream Protestants were characteristically American in deciding that they wanted religion to comfort, coddle, and soothe. They did not want their religion to prod them into a higher ethic if it would interfere with their getting wealth and happiness.

As the Great Depression of the 1930s became a dim recollection, the love of wealth and the rising expectations of typical mainstream Protestants found them ready to lie down at ease in Zion. Prophetic concerns for the plight of the poor were acceptable. What was not acceptable was pointing to the facts that the poor were being kept in their poverty by the attitudes of the middle and upper classes—mainstream Protestants! We cannot hope to understand the contemporary mainstream Protestants unless we clearly recognize how effectively a psychologized religion served our intensified materialism, which was excited by an age of plenty for a majority and deprivation for a minority.

All over America the church leaders, mainstream and others, were up against Christians' demand that they be soothed and assured that whatever their way of living might be, "God loves and accepts you as you are." Intended by some preachers to mean that God values a sinner, this unfortunate phrase was widely interpreted to mean that anything is approved by God, whose love is so generous that we have no cause to worry about God or what God will do to us. The ancient prophets and our tradition do not understand God this way. They insist that God holds us responsible to establish justice in the land.

Norman Vincent Peale is the most successful practitioner of psychologizing religion. With his "power of positive thinking" Peale avoids theology and biblical scholarship. He is a superior agent for a psychologized form of Christian faith. It is important to understand his origins. He is the true American mainstream Protestant—now retired but valued by millions of Americans who have been helped by him to be very positive about everything.

Peale was born on May 31, 1898 in Bowersville, Greene County, Ohio. His father was trained to be a doctor, served as Health Commissioner in Milwaukee, and became a Methodist pastor after he recovered from an illness that had threatened his life. To his last day he believed that God had saved him from death so that he could be a pastor instead of a physician. Peale's autobiography speaks glowingly of his Ohio boyhood and his family relationships.[2]

Norman Vincent Peale received a good education and became pastor of Marble Collegiate Church in New York City on October 2, 1932. It was a ripe time for somebody to take an optimistic view in a gloomy city. Peale's psychologization of religion met the mood of the depression in New York City. At a time when the entire world was deeply involved in economic collapse which threatened all but a very few people, Peale affirmed the "power of positive thinking." He was not a scholar in either psychology or theology, but he had a feel for the things people wanted to hear and a distinct flare for showmanship which made him stand out.

This metaphor, the "power of positive thinking," holds power for two reasons. First, it is very true that much of the trouble we think we are in can be handled if we just take it by the forelock and go to work on it. Positive thinking is, perhaps, the solution to more than half of our failures to succeed in making money. Second, it holds power because it justifies our deep-seated mainstream Protestant greediness. If there ever was an emphasis on doing for one's self first, "the power of positive thinking" is that emphasis. It is not without interest that Norman Vincent Peale's autobiography is a rather gleeful report on success in making money and winning friendships among the powerful.[3]

Although Peale is generously criticized and sometimes ridiculed by some pastors, he is imitated everywhere. In only a few instances is his skill as a salesman of a viewpoint surpassed. With Peale's help, psychologization of religion thrives with real vitality all over the land. Of course, all preachers are not equally skilled in presenting the new religion that cloaks Christianity, but even preachers in tiny hamlets and crossroads bend their best efforts to help people adjust to life.

The influence of Peale is impossible to measure because it was such an expansive and joyous assurance that all is right with the world so long as you just keep on thinking that things are all right. It was an affirmation of each individual's egocentric interests. It was a culmination of the mainstream Protestant drive toward success in materialistic pursuits, and it caught the American people well prepared to accept it. That Peale's shallow view of life was undermining the Christian faith and weakening the ministry of the churches to deeper human needs was seldom noticed.

Most leaders now find ways to avoid asking people to change the social order. We hope to help people become well adjusted to life. In the late 1930s, Bishop Francis John McConnell, a Methodist, published an article in *The Christian Advocate* on "The Peril of Being Well Adjusted." The title of that article awoke me to the dangerous trend. Perhaps our churches would be better off today if all of us had taken Bishop McConnell's warning to heart.

The psychologizing of religion witnessed an important development when Carl Rogers became a dominant influence in theological schools with his emphasis on "non-directional counseling." Drawing on the best methods of holding the psychiatric interview, Rogers extended the emphasis to train pastors to be better listeners. The main role of the pastor would be to move very slowly and let troubled souls discover solutions or answers to problems by drawing on their own insights and resources. This was an important correction to the tendencies of preachers to impose their views on others.

Rogers and others who came to the front in advocating the kind of pastoral care that encourages personal autonomy have done much to improve Christian ministry to the distressed soul of our times. Their emphasis seems close to the kind of human relationship projected by the portrayal of Jesus in the synoptic gospels where he is, more often than not, seen as non-authoritarian. However, it must be recognized that in other references Jesus is depicted as sternly the opposite. In this connection, some advocates of non-directional counseling stereotype Jesus without warrant.

However valuable the non-directive approach in pastoral care may be, it can be a disaster in pastoral leadership of a congregation. When the pastor steps out of the leadership role in preaching and church administration and becomes non-directive, the vacuum is often filled with strong personalities from the laity. These strong personalities may be literally pushed into leadership roles by the church members who see the need for stronger leadership. Sometimes these strong personalities may have disciplined themselves to be very democratic; sometimes the reverse may be true. When the pastor is not seen as a leader, the church organization will find a leader to meet its needs. Many local churches know the difficulties that develop when non-directional pastoral leadership results in confusion.

There is always some danger in mainstream Protestantism that a strong but self-willed lay person may take advantage of a pastor's non-directional inclination. It is a legitimate role of the pastor to neither be a dictator nor allow anyone else to become a dictator over the congregation. I have pointed to the distinct feature of American mainstream Protestantism with laity in tension with the clergy, both seeking control of the church organization. When non-directive pastors abandon their full obligation to sustain the tension, they cease to be leaders.

The net result of our pastors carrying their non-directional methods into the pulpit and organizational meetings is a church that gradually enjoys being non-directional. If a strong lay leader takes control and becomes a dictator, which sometimes happens, the tendency will be to make a non-directional response. There is a certain loveliness, a peace-and-quiet note, in non-directional relationships that can be very dangerous under certain circumstances.

This great problem of a clergy trained to be non-directional is not generally recognized because it is not painful. There is nothing as pleasant as the company of a non-directional person who seems wholly dedicated to compassionate understanding of what we say. All of us enjoy being understood. The nicest people we meet are non-directional, and those who complain about such nice people cannot be easily understood by any of us. My colleagues who are fully committed to being non-directional are very easy to get along with. Unfortunately, I learn very little from them because they never challenge me. They seem to be without opinions or convictions.

The resulting mainstream Protestant church in America is a harmless pigeon with its psychologized Christianity and its non-directional clergy. Our clergy are thoroughly professionalized, and this gives rise to another problem. The mainstream clergy have increasingly abandoned the streets to the Mormons, the fundamentalists, and the odd sects. We announce our office hours and wait for troubled souls to seek us out. We have watched the physicians and lawyers achieve professional status with people in their waiting rooms. We must have ours, too.

Lost to our motives is the thought that we will hunt for atheists, pregnant teenagers, hustling money-makers, bored college professors, anxious parents, and that great host of Americans who have not been in a church for years and would hardly know what to do if they had the courage to walk through our front doors one Sunday morning. It is in that great throng that our future lies. But they will never come to see us in our study, although we would welcome them and would work hard as their non-directional counselor if they would only come to seek our help.

When I was at the peak of my concentration on psychologizing our faith, I was in a downtown church where I held office hours and had a sufficient number of people asking for appointments to make me feel that I was really doing the job. After about ten years of devoted service to this method, I decided to review the situation and discovered that I was spending most of my time and energy with a surprisingly small number of people. Furthermore, an honest examination of the facts led me to the conclusion that these might not be the people who most needed a pastor. (Experienced pastors will immediately recognize this problem.)

I was forced to figure out a new way to carry out my pastoral task. By that time the social configuration had become rigidly urbanized. Not even a pastor could walk down the street and knock on doors to get a response. Arrangements to see strangers or church members had to be made in advance. Furthermore, people would invariably ask, "Why do you want to see me?"

Even my church members would ask this. If they were in some kind of trouble, then they were all the more suspicious when the pastor called on the telephone to make an appointment to see them. They wondered who had tattled.

All pastors know this problem which is encountered with their own church members; just think how much more complex the task is when we call to make an appointment with a stranger. The recent innovations of computerized uses of the telephone—with callers selling everything from gold mine stock to magazines—has made the telephone an enemy. A pastor has to recognize this cultural shift and surmount the obstacles.

When I finally worked out a method of approach for making advance appointments with a church member or with strangers, I then had to abandon the concept of non-directional pastoral counseling in favor of something more appropriate. This is not the place to expand on that method because it would take us too far afield, but it was essentially an approach to people based on the general proposition that I wanted to become acquainted and to learn more about what others were thinking. This has its non-directional background, but it puts the pastor in a different role. It worked for me. The fondest recollections I have are of times when I was allowed to meet with self-proclaimed atheists who were subsequently baptized and brought into the Christian community.

I had to break away from a limited conception of the pastoral role that had grown naturally out of my training and personal interest in the psychologization of religion. Until I learned how to get back into the streets, I was not doing much, if anything, to bring new members into my mainstream church. Furthermore, my church members were not doing anything either until I was able to tell them how to do what I was doing. That's the way it is. That's the way it will be.

We mainstream church leaders psychologize religion for serious reasons. We want to help our people deal with life's problems. We are determined to be good Christians, faithful pastors, and responsible church leaders. It is only now beginning to be clear to us that we have been avoiding our responsibility to be theologians in residence. We have left theology for the professional theologians, and they have abandoned us. They dwell in a land where they speak their own language and enjoy their own customs of discourse. We have abandoned biblical studies to the scholars, and they are so far ahead of us that we can hardly see their tracks in the dusty literature that they publish in their professional journals.

Our success in psychologizing religion permitted us to avoid theology until now. We were not jolted into facing the realities by warnings from theologians and sociologists. When the "God is Dead" theologians hit the front page of national news weeklies, we were untouched. Not until our membership ranks began to decline year after year did we awaken to see how deeply we were into lasting trouble.

In the previous chapter I referred briefly to the work of Charles Y. Glock and Rodney Stark (see chapter 1, endnote 10). Their extensive research convincingly showed that the mainstream Protestants were losing members because their theology wouldn't support their social ethic. The few leaders who knew anything about Glock and Stark might have concluded they could easily resolve that problem by slowing down and going quiet on social issues. Leaders who may not have known about the work of Glock and Stark probably sensed what was happening and knew, without being told, why it was happening.

What Glock and Stark had done in their research was only a beginning. Had they continued they would have been able to confirm what both Gallup and Harris polls continue to show: a decline in the number of church members who believe in the supernatural interventions of God into private and social affairs of the human race. Yet these same polls reveal many inside and outside of the churches who make amazing, if not preposterous, claims about supernatural activities—from flying saucers to personal visits from St. Ignatius.

Cults making bizarre claims about connections with supernatural powers spring up all over the land. One of the more recent examples is a spontaneous outbreak of New Age publications that make extravagant claims about healings, accomplishments, and triumph over death. In the theological vacuum formed by the vanishing theologies of tradition, the crackpots are taking over with psychology fused to supernaturalism, and they take the stratosphere for their limit. While the mainstream Protestants are less inclined to believe in periodic interventions of supernatural powers, the people outside of the churches seem to have become more and more inclined to believe in supernatural intervention in human affairs.

This is an interesting and very complex phenomena needing careful investigation. My own interpretation is cautious, but I see in this a reluctance to affirm religious experience of God in ordinary processes and events. There is a tendency in our culture to hold back from developing a theology that helps us to make real sense out of the ordinary wonders of daily life.

PSYCHOLOGIZING WORSHIP

Another negative feature accompanies the psychologization of our faith. Our services of divine worship are turned into social gatherings where the coffee break after the benediction is often valued more than the hymns, prayers, liturgies, and sermon. This apathy toward worship has been lamented in clergy journals over a period of at least two generations. Every trick imaginable has been proposed to make the services of worship socially attractive. Any person who travels across the United States and visits a different mainstream church every Sunday will see the ravaged hour. Take some of the United Methodists as an illustration. In the new hymnal issued in 1989 one finds "An Order of Sunday Worship Using the Basic Pattern." It suggests that while the people are gathering they should visit; make announcements; rehearse congregational music; or have informal prayer, singing, or testimony. Quiet meditation and prayer seem to be suggested as an afterthought.

Psychologization has two main effects on our gathering for worship. First of all, it turns us away from the meditative focus on God and trains us to put our focus on the workings of our minds. We interiorize faith and lose that yearning to touch the Infinite Glory that surrounds all of us to make us one family. The poetry of knowing the Tremendous Mystery, in some small measure, is sacrificed in favor of forming theories about our feelings and thoughts. We do not gather to hear ourselves called by God into a higher level of service. We "go to church" to get help in achieving goals we have established for ourselves and consider to be essential.

Fundamentalist Christianity often goes further than mainstream Protestantism in this regard. It has become routine for fundamentalist preachers, especially charismatics, to promise health, wealth, and happiness to people who do specific things to please God. Too often the things that are said to please God and secure divine favor have to do with money given to the fundamentalist church.

Mainstream Protestants are more restrained when it comes to raising money. They seldom promise eternal rewards or punishment in exchange for dedicated stewardship of wealth. As a consequence, they may not always raise as much money per capita as the charismatic fundamentalists do on television and in other places. But there are no signs that mainstream Protestants will exact tribute money for peace of mind or salvation of one's eternal soul. Mainstream Protestants sustain a significant ministry to distressed people of the world by appealing to their generosity and Christian dedication. Even so, it is fair to ask whether our worldwide programs of ministry can be sustained if we continue to psychologize our religion.

The second effect on our service of public worship of God wrought by psychologizing religion is the evaporation from our lives of a deep sense of awe and eternity. When religion is reduced to psychology, science provides the sole understanding of the world around us. The doctrine of evolution has been accepted widely to mean that human life is more or less an accident on earth. The birth and death of stars is regularly announced and taken to mean that earth is a mere speck with an impressive history soon to be extinguished. All in all, the sciences contribute a great flow of data to feed into our reduction of religion to a sophisticated form of psychology we employ to help us struggle onward to the end of our solitary life: a life that ends with death.

BEYOND PSYCHOLOGIZATION

Could we have done anything else but psychologize religion following the turn of the century when our theology began to be inadequate for our needs? It seems almost inevitable that what actually happened simply had to happen. We mainstream Protestants were vital, strong, committed to human life, and we sustained strong impulses to serve human need. With a failing theology, a promising psychological fix was something like a godsend after about 1930.

Today we can go beyond psychologization. One might too easily conclude that all we have to do is announce a new theology and sound the trumpet, calling all souls to a serious inquiry into new biblical scholarship. Unfortunately, it will not be that easy. We should pay serious attention in mainline Protestantism to the rich contributions now being made by anthropology and phenomenology. Both of these fields of learning have much to say about religious experience that promises a wider view of how human beings experience God, just as psychology enriched our pastoral ministry earlier in this century.

The College of William and Mary, Department of Anthropology, has issued two volumes dealing with Christian missionaries and their encounters with people of other cultures.[4] No American Christian church leader could read these two studies without feeling drawn in the direction of trying to feel the holiness of all things: trees, oceans, rivers, human life in its various kinds, and all that supports its continuance. To see the holiness of nature and life is not to fall into shallow pantheism. Jesus was not a pantheist when he spoke of mustard seeds, vines, soils, and similar things to evoke an image of the Kingdom of God in the hearts and minds of listeners. We Christians need to understand life as a whole instead of seeing it by breaking it into parts.

The people to whom our missionaries were sent often had what our Christian emissaries lacked: a sense of awe and a feeling for eternity. I am not saying that studying primitive people will tell us very much about ourselves, but the approach of anthropology to our American situation in life will tell us much that psychology has overlooked.

There is another open door that is beckoning to us as we begin to reconsider our theology and our uses of the Bible. While we were so busily dedicated to psychologizing religion in America as an alternative to our fading theology, there were strengthening developments in philosophy that provoked the suspicions of many mainstream Christians. The existentialists emerged in poetry, fiction, and politics. They ridiculed our extreme rationalism and, at the same time, saddled us with the burden that human beings are responsible for their own choices. Heidegger, Jaspers, Marcel, and Sartre rejected our theology and our psychologizing. They seem to have understood, before we theologians did, that life cannot be adequately understood by analysis alone. After the existentialists came the phenomenologists.

The phenomenologists consider Edmund Gustav Albrecht Husserl (1859-1938) to be their founder. He began his career by saying that all logic is psychological, but he spent his life refuting that position. Instead, he argued, "pure logic" is contrary to "psychologism." The stirrings of phenomenology were hardly noticed by pastors and Christian leaders in America. But there was an affinity between the anthropologists and the phenomenologists following 1900. This affinity became very real in Friedrich Heiler (1892-1967), the Marburg historian of religion.

Only recently has Heiler become available to those of us who are not easily at home in the German language. The best contribution to date is Peter McKenzie's splendid adaptation of Heiler, which is published under the title *The Christians: Their Practices and Beliefs.* The opening lines of the Introduction to this very readable book explain how phenomenology applies to the issues being discussed here:

> In this work, Christianity will be presented, I believe for the first time, in detailed phenomenological form. It will not be the approach of theology, though use will be made of theology in the form of religious concepts, e.g. creation or revela-

tion. . . . It is also not a history of Christianity although extensive historical material will be found in its pages. It is to be distinguished, again, from sociology or psychology of religion but these also will not be altogether neglected. . . . What, then, is phenomenology of religion? Very briefly, phenomenology of religion makes use of the materials provided by the history of religions, theology, sociology and psychology of religion, as well as its own direct observations. Out of these materials significant religious phenomena disclose or manifest themselves to the interpreter.[5]

The anthropologists and phenomenologists realized a long time ago that we were confused when we displaced religion with psychology in our mainstream Protestant preaching and praxis. At the same time, these very same anthropologists and phenomenologists might seriously mislead us if we fail to make clear the distinguishing features of the Christian religion. What the anthropologists and phenomenologists can help us do is to see more clearly the nature of religious experience. We should not confine ourselves to psychology as the only discipline for understanding religion.

A NEW OUTLOOK

Although for two decades we have preferred to go deeply into psychologization of religion with a focus on becoming well adjusted, this may have a fortuitous turn. Although digging into the unconscious didn't bring the answers we hoped for, we have learned that our ordinary human existence ties into the greater sweep of earth and all that lies beyond. In a definite way, our forty or fifty-year emphasis on the care of the soul has produced a people who will insist that any theology will not neglect this important aspect of existence.

There is emerging a new mainstream Protestant mentality. This new mentality insists that taking care of our minds and bodies is our basic task, but we cannot take care of our minds and bodies unless we also nurture our social environment and our entire ecological environment. Although we never intended it to come out as it has, we have built into mainstream Protestantism the readiness for a theology of the immediate immanence of God and its accompanying ecological ethic.

ROLE OF THEOLOGY

Religion can be wrong-headed. It is a major role of theology to keep religion intelligently on the track of saying what seems to be most true about God, the world, and human life. I have stated that we in mainstream Protestantism made a mistake because we did not know that we were psychologizing the Christian faith. Now, as we go forward, we must be careful to distinguish between religion and theology.

Theology is its own distinctive discipline. It is the steersman, the hand on the guiding oar, of our religious response to the phenomena of existence. Theology is concerned with our understanding of the world and our role in its processes. Theology goes beyond the task we assign to psychology because it is concerned with much more than how our mental and emotional states take place or interact. Theology goes beyond anthropology, phenomenology, and philosophy because it inevitably entangles us in two considerations that are uniquely theological.

The first of these two considerations is that theology is concerned with the meaning of human life which must be carried out in a vast web of uncertainty and consequence. Every day of our life is spent in a succession of events we cannot entirely control. Our existence is consequential, and this gives meaning to our lives; but we cannot predict with absolute certainty how events will turn out. Theology helps us to face this dilemma. In this connection, William Henry Bernhardt speaks of theology as a commitment to realism: "It is better to live in terms of verified probabilities than of unverified certainties."[6]

The second consideration is that a realistic and convincing theology must take with full seriousness the meaning of our death, that unwelcome but inevitable event in every person's history. Death cannot be psychologized because it is that inevitable capstone demanding reflection on life's meanings.

Continuous consequential experience with sustained uncertainty until we die are the two most pressing and vexing concerns nestled in the heart of theology. We try to phrase our understanding of these vexations in our theology, but our theology is not our religion. It is a tool of our religion. That is to say that Christianity as our religion is not a theology—it is a way of living that is sustained by a theology.

Theology is our way of talking about faith in God. Christian faith is a way of living in the world where uncertainty is tied to consequence and sin and death are as real as holiness and birth. A realistic theology puts the Christian into the world as a creature with a way of ultimate meaning for her or his life.

When we psychologize our faith, we internalize our vision and we dwarf the mystery of the human soul. Traditional theology no longer has a sufficient reach for our minds and hearts which are heavily burdened by new knowledge of our world we have not yet assimilated. Our theology has not been big enough for our intellectual and emotional needs.

Our taking refuge in the psychologizing of religion was understandable. We needed quick relief from psychic suffering. It also fit hand-in-glove with our American passion for self-gratification. We have been instructed by psychology while we have been misled by its charms. We were led astray and we failed to formulate a theology that would permit us to talk about God in a language that enables all of us to make sense out of our unpredictable but consequential world. Caught in the whirlwind of new knowledge and flooded by a burgeoning technology born out of advanced sciences, we mainstream Protestants did not realize how fast the world was moving. We had helped to produce the very factors that entrapped us after the turn of this century. We have been caught by what we chased. Now we must amend our ways, for there are richer resources for the nurture of our souls.

Everywhere in our great land people are yearning for something better than psychologized religion and more convincing than fundamentalistic theology. Many American Christians who still support fundamentalistic theology may be ready to turn away from it. We are in a new era and we will require a Christian theology to help us make sense out of our lives which are locked into uncertainty and consequence. We are yearning for a theology to sustain a whole ecological ethic which holds every atom precious and recognizes all forms of life and material substance as a gift from God. We hunger for a theology that will save our souls and also conserve this very beautiful planet—our only home for this life.

People want and deserve more help in living, but the mainstream Protestant churches are malnourished and growing weaker.

C H A P T E R
III

THE MALNOURISHED CHURCH

What metaphor shall we use in talking about the contemporary mainstream Protestant churches? Dean Kelley recently used a mechanical metaphor and said, "It is out of steam." Many pastors use the metaphor of a living organism and say, "It is dead." I will refer to the church as a social organism. I doubt if we are dying, but we are definitely low in energy. I find it most helpful to think of us as a malnourished social organism. I will show in this chapter how our health depends on nourishment provided by vital beliefs. I will argue that we suffer from an improper diet of outworn theology, literalistic biblical interpretation, and psychologized religion.

Those of us who have been assigned responsibility to feed and take care of the flock have not been providing the necessary intellectual and emotional resources. We are not to be judged harshly for our failure. We were convinced that our theology and biblical teachings were valid enough to be something like eternal truth. Our history convinced us that our success proved we were right. Most of us find it difficult to believe, even now, that the doctrines that served mainstream Protestantism so well in the first two centuries of American development are no longer sufficient. It is not unusual for even a good nutritionist to fail to understand when a changed organism needs a new diet.

THE CHURCH AS A SOCIAL ORGANIZATION

We failed to see the needs of our churches because we did not pay enough attention to the fact that as social organisms our churches behave in ways similar to other social organizations. As such, sociology and other disciplines that study social behavior can provide helpful insights into workings of our churches. We do not usually speak of the church as a social organization. We have other metaphors that carry connotations that seem more churchly or religious. Although we may feel a bit uncomfortable with the metaphor of the church as a social organization, I will draw upon it to illustrate certain things about mainstream Protestantism that we must see more clearly if we are to gather new strength. The more critically the reader examines the way I will use the metaphor, the better we will move together to see the facts which are elusive because we are dealing with an extremely complex entity—the church, with a lower case *c*. I think of the Church with a capital *C* as the Holy Catholic Church I yearn for, while at the same time I struggle to understand the little *c* church I must live with and try to serve. The church as a social organization is different from other social organizations in many ways, but the church is subject to the same conditions that all other social organizations encounter; it lives as other social organizations must live. If it fails or falters, then we must look at it in much the same way that we look at any other social organization.

An instructive description of how social organizations live and have their being is provided by Daniel Katz and Robert L. Kahn.[1] They found that people are held together in social organizations by three things:

(1) There must be *beliefs* about appropriate and required behavior shared by members of the organization.
(2) There must be convincing proof that a majority of members of the group agree with the *beliefs*.
(3) The members of the group must be kept aware that there is group support for the *beliefs*.

The central word in these three things that tie people together is *beliefs*. It may seem at first that it should be very easy to know what the beliefs are that bond people together into an organization. On reflection, it turns out that it is extremely difficult to know what people believe. Even with the best of polls we may not get at the real descriptions of belief. When it comes to matters of religion, we soon know that a belief is a very complicated thing. What a person professes to believe is often very far from what that person really believes. Most of us hardly know what we ourselves believe on some subjects of real importance. To talk about an organization of people who hold the same beliefs about required behavior for group members can be a tricky conversation. Leaders of organizations invariably fail when they make too many wrong assumptions about what their members really and truly do believe.

Some leaders happen to be very systematic in investigation, and others are just plain lucky in knowing with fair accuracy what the members in their particular organizations believe. The simpler the goals of the organization, the easier it is to know what beliefs are important and to ignore all those beliefs that are not. The leader of a political party must be very sharp in discerning what the party members believe in common, yet leading a political party is easier than leading a church. The political organization may have a single belief that it requires: support our candidate. Measuring the strength of support for a belief of that nature is difficult enough, but it can be done. A church organization is another matter, because a church is formed around a belief structure as complicated as one is likely to find. Church leaders must be more skillful in handling belief matters than leaders of other social organizations whose bonding belief systems are easier to interpret and understand.

Katz and Kahn note how organizations falter if the leadership does not know when the members of the group are shifting their beliefs. It is inevitable that what the members of a group believe will change in some degree with the passage of time. But all organizations have built-in controls over changes in beliefs. One of the primary functions of rules, regulations, constitutions, and creeds is to keep changes in belief at a minimum. No organization can thrive without a certain amount of continuity in belief. It is also true that human beings are resistant to belief controls, and members in organizations do change their beliefs in spite of organizational controls.

Real trouble is afoot when the members of an organization undergo experiences that cause erosion in their beliefs almost against their will and, to a great extent, without open discussion. It is possible that widespread shifting of belief will take place throughout an organization if there are substantial influences affecting all or most of the individuals in the organization. Even though most people may not deliberately change their beliefs, circumstances requiring them to make adjustments in their beliefs will come whether they invite those circumstances or not. Our beliefs may change without our awareness or even, to some degree, against our will.

When our beliefs become different from the prevailing beliefs in an organization, we may or may not drop out. What people do in circumstances of belief differences within an organization to which they belong is an unexplored question. Have people dropped out of the mainstream Protestant churches because they no longer believe what they are being told that they should believe? Do people often find that they are dropping out almost against their own will? Do many people stay away from the churches because they assume that they cannot believe what they will be asked to believe? When people lose interest in the church, is it because their beliefs have become disconnected?

We do not have solid information to answer these questions. It is extremely difficult to get data on what people deeply believe about God, prayer, moral choice, and eternity. What we do know is that people are held, in part, within organizational boundaries by a bonding of beliefs. We may properly assume that when beliefs change significantly, the belief bonding system weakens. Without strong bonding of their beliefs, people drop out; and those who have never belonged to the organization soon learn what is going on. People are not drawn to affiliate with organizations whose members are dropping out. Mainstream Protestants have a real problem on this point: with declines in membership, mainstream Protestants do not attract new members into their ranks. We have a reputation of being in decline, and that hurts us. Prospective members wonder what ails us. They probably sense our lack of group conviction.

Resurgent Fundamentalism

During the 1980s, when the loss of members from mainstream Protestantism continued as a real cause for concern, each denomination suddenly discovered within its organizational life a resurgence of fundamentalism. These various internal movements had strong leaders with determined views. They pointed to membership decline and offered a remedy: return to the theology of fundamentalism, restore biblical literalism, and forget the Social Gospel in favor of an emphasis on "traditional values." This latter plea was actually an invitation to turn away from the higher and more exacting demands of an ethic that includes all of God's creation. Such an ecological ethic includes every concern pertaining to the holiness of human life and the protective caring for the whole earth and its varying forms of life. There has been a national anxiety about gross sexual indulgence, violence, and family disruption on a wide scale. An ethic of "traditional values" promises correction of these evils. However, the real appeal of the new fundamentalists is certainty of beliefs.

In The United Methodist Church, this resurgent fundamentalism calls itself the "Good News Movement." In the United Church of Christ, a similar internal group of dissenters calls itself the "Biblical Witness Fellowship." All of the mainline Protestant denominations found dissenting organizations within their ranks. They are thorns in the flesh of the mainstream Protestant bodies. In each denomination they voice identical appeals: return to what we once proclaimed. This is their open confession that they believe the mainstream Protestant belief system to be in disarray, decline, or apostasy.

The leaders of these dissenting groups inside the denominational organizations obviously believe that the established leadership is failing to gauge accurately the deterioration of the belief system. They are correct. The mainstream leadership has lost touch with the beliefs of a large proportion of the members in the local churches. But the dissenting leaders are also out of touch with all who are not fundamentalists. The people who are dropping out of the mainstream Protestant ranks refuse to join forces with the fundamentalists who are still inside the mainstream church. Nor can these people walk out and hunt up a thriving fundamentalist church to join. Millions of mainstream Protestants have quietly dropped out or became inactive. Adults who have never belonged to any church know what is happening and are influenced by it. Psychologized religion was not able to hold people in the church, and it was not able to win people to join the church. When a church is without vital beliefs to share, it is destined to decline.

Conflict Without Compromise

In the face of internal discord and a declining membership, all of the mainline Protestant bodies did the same thing, each in its own way. They tried to find a common meeting ground where established leadership and dissident leadership could stand together on matters of belief. It is of more than passing importance that in each of the mainstream denominations the conflict was not openly stated as a conflict over beliefs. Instead, it was described as a conflict over the missionary activities of the respective churches, both at home and overseas.

However, the real conflict between the fundamentalists and established liberal leadership inside the mainstream Protestant ranks is over who will control the organization *and* determine its beliefs. It is impossible to separate the drive to control the organization from an equally hard drive to control the belief system. This management of power is common to all religious leaders. The fundamentalists want to control the church organization, and their claims for the right to control are based on the argument that their beliefs are true and correct. When the opposing leadership tries to open up a common ground of understanding, both sides know what is at stake: power.

The dissident fundamentalists inside the mainstream churches know that they are in the minority, but their strong beliefs convince them that they must win the power struggle. All efforts to achieve a common understanding are bound to fail. This should be known at the outset, because when there is a clash between belief systems inside an organization, there is no room for compromise. Leaders of conflicting belief systems cannot compromise, because to do so means sacrificing their leadership status. When belief systems collide, a power struggle ensues.

The established mainstream Protestant leadership knows that we cannot go back to the fundamentalism and biblical literalism being advocated by the dissident groups that are challenging our denominations. The dissident leaders know that they cannot abandon the belief systems that they are convinced are revealed truth from God. Because both the established leaders and the dissident leaders belong to the same social organization, the struggle to control the belief system is also a struggle to determine who will control the organization—the church.

A sample illustration of a futile attempt to reach compromise of belief system conflict is provided by the United Methodists. They voted in 1984 to hold meetings involving establishment leaders and dissident leaders. They assigned several bishops to work with the General Board of Global Ministries and charged them with responsibility to hold open dialogue with the "Good News" leaders. After four years of trying to find a common meeting ground, the bishops reported in 1988 that these efforts had been fruitless. No common meeting ground on beliefs could be found. They said that further efforts at dialogue should not be attempted. This was clear admission that the organized life of The United Methodist Church had a dispute it could not resolve. It was also an admission that a clash of belief systems inside a church organization is, in the final analysis, a power struggle as well.

Many experienced church leaders knew before dialogue was attempted that the differences would not be resolved. But it is necessary to go through the ritual of seeming to try to resolve conflicts between beliefs even when the eventual deadlock is predictable. Internal conflicts inside the church are supposed to be reconciled with joyous conclusions. History tells us how rare this is. But the contemporary predicament of mainstream

Protestantism tells us how necessary it is that we find ways to reach a creative solution to the conflict we have over our beliefs and the power to control the organization.

Although we who are charged with mainstream Protestant leadership are painfully aware of the unrest in our organizations, there is no evidence suggesting that we are ready at this time to face the truth about our troubles with beliefs. What we know for sure is that our organization is not only weakening but also will continue to decline. Something is happening to our abilities to do what we are charged to do. We are no longer leading our churches. We are trying to hold the fort while trusting that solutions to our problems will somehow come. I am ready to argue for a method of engagement that will bring us to creative solutions. But we must first probe more extensively the nature of a malnourished church.

SYMPTOMS OF A MALNOURISHED CHURCH

In the interests of trying to understand more exactly what a malnourished church is going through, I have identified several symptoms. I am calling these features symptoms of an ailment: they are not the ailment itself, which is the basic malnutrition of our church's belief systems. When all or most of these symptoms are present, we can be fairly certain that we are dealing with a malnourished church. Drawing upon the metaphor of physical organisms, we can say that these symptoms may not be painful. Because they are not painful, we may miss seeing them as serious warning signals that we are in deep trouble.

1. Restructuring is sometimes useful, but quite often it is a sure sign of a faltering organization. A change of structure is always announced in glowing terms, promising great things to come. Large sums of money spent on travel, job changes, and even relocation of offices seem to prove the seriousness of the undertakings. During the first twenty years of mainstream Protestant decline (1950-1970), the restructuring of mainstream denominations was contagious. Restructuring generates a kind of football-stadium enthusiasm. Leaders are excited by the prospects that the realignments of power may yield promotions

they want. The leaders who have no chance of being promoted enjoy the exercise of influence and power. When experienced church leaders look back at all of their restructuring experiences, they often admit that little was accomplished. Restructuring is a pleasant symptom of organizational weakness that is often left without diagnosis. It is a rare church leader who sees restructuring as a symptom, a danger signal—that the church is suffering malnourishment of its belief system.

2. Union of organizations is a symptom of their mutual difficulties. Robust, thriving churches fend off unification efforts. A robust church may assimilate a weaker church in much the same way that a large fish may swallow a smaller one. But unification in mainstream Protestantism, whether desirable or undesirable, is a definite sign that serious problems of strength and vitality are pressing for solution. Sometimes there has been a history of strife that has caused divisions which need to be healed. The dispute over slavery caused a major division in mainstream Protestant bodies, and union of separated bodies has been slow to come. It is significant that a major ingredient in producing unification of Southern and Northern branches within several American denominations has been the need of each side for certain strengths that the other side could bring into the union. One of the marked features of mainstream Protestantism today is the cry for church unity, and this cry is issuing out of a real consciousness of diminishing vitality in the separated mainstream Protestant organizations.

3. Meetings to define goals are another symptom. A thriving organization knows what its goals are. A malnourished church will show uncertainty about goals. When there is a sustained emphasis on redefining goals, one may be almost certain that there is an underlying problem that is even more serious than the lack of clearly stated goals. Experienced church leaders soon learn that meetings to redefine goals are actually meetings where people do a lot of worrying about their organizational strength. Malnourished churches announce meetings to clarify goals when the real concern is the inability to move toward any significant goal. Of course, this isn't openly admitted. It may not even be recognized. A meeting announced

as an occasion for worrying about the vitality of the organization would let the cat out of the bag.

4. Meetings to amend previously defined goals are a very definite signal that the organization is suffering malnutrition of its belief systems. When a church cannot reach a clear decision about its goals, it will still continue to believe that failure to clarify goals is what it really lacks. The people will meet to amend previously adopted goals and to define new ones. The emphasis here is on the phenomenon of repeated gatherings to talk about goals. Some local churches and some denominations spend years on goal definition, with each successive meeting amending the goals adopted by the previous meeting. Hardly anyone ever notices that goals are extensions of beliefs. It is almost unheard of to learn that a church has called a meeting to reexamine its belief system. However, if form follows function in architecture, then action follows belief in religion. A church that is showing confusion about its organizational goals is suffering from a seriously disordered belief system. Redefining goals is a fine way to avoid discussing beliefs that either do or do not call for a particular goal.

5. We may be certain that our organization is malnourished when we select mediocre people for positions of top responsibility. Weakening churches do not want strong leaders; they want leaders who will not make things worse. By *mediocrity* I mean average, medium, moderate, cautious. There may not be such a thing as a "group mind," but there is a peculiar quality about groups of people which suggests that organizations have a common outlook on some things. When people in an organization somehow sense that they are losing their vitality and strength of purpose, they look for someone to rescue them without rocking the boat. The best protection against boat-rocking leaders is the person who points backward to the "good old days." Mediocre leaders help the people to escape from challenges that might require them to run risks now and then. Strong organizations are eager for challenges. Weak or malnourished organizations hesitate to run the risks of being innovative, creative, venturesome. Mediocrity opens no new frontiers. It holds the fort with mediocre leaders in charge.

When a church consistently chooses top leaders from the ranks of the mediocre, it shows its malnourished condition. It knows that it cannot run the risks of energetic innovation and movement.

6. When a church is languishing, a new tone emerges in the financial reports. There is a repeated refrain that "we did as well as we did last year." Money is important. Anything we may wish to do to help people requires money, no matter how many people volunteer their services. The mainstream Protestants have adopted the habit of being thankful if their income this year has kept up with inflation. For example, the "most American" of the churches (The United Methodist Church) reported that its total income of 1988 was 6 percent greater than it was in 1987 (9 percent better in 1989 over 1988). This report did not say that inflation accounted for 4.5 percent of that 1988 increase, leaving a net gain of 1.5 percent at best. During the same period, this denomination lost about 70,000 members. But the point here is that a malnourished church will make good news out of breaking even. A robust church in good health would be able to report gains on all fronts. Or, if big losses were suffered in membership or income, these would be attributed to real causes justifying the losses.

7. Another symptom of malnourishment in the mainstream church is the inability to be self-critical in the sense of admitting the flaws that are real. Every physician has patients who engage in denial. Patients who deny their ailments often make themselves worse by doing the wrong things to their bodies and to their minds. The inability to be self-critical is rooted in the realistic awareness that a weakened belief system may collapse altogether if challenged in the wrong way. There seems to be a fear that loosening an old foundation stone here and there will cause the entire church structure to collapse. This is a very serious matter that we will explore as we go along. When the foundation has become weak, there may be no alternative to essential reconstruction.

8. The final symptom of a malnourished church is its inability to take needed nourishment abruptly. Abrupt corrections in diet can be fatal. A malnourished church with its

deprived and weakened beliefs is in no condition to handle the rough fodder of new ideas and the substance of enriched experiences in a hurry. Abruptly loading the malnourished mainstream churches with a new diet of rich food will do more harm than good. Although all of these symptoms go together, whenever we try to understand our churches, this reference to the inability of a malnourished organization to handle an abrupt change of diet must be given emphasis. I do not believe that it is either necessary or possible to do what we must do and to get it done in haste. The mainstream Protestant movement in America is still a very strong, vital church. That it is weakening is easy to prove. It is equally easy to prove that nobody ever helped an organization to recover its vitality by trying to ram a belief system down its throat. Our leadership task calls for something far more complicated than learning how to shout new ideas in a louder voice.

LEADERSHIP IN A MALNOURISHED CHURCH

Nurturing the belief system calls for great skill, and we who hold leadership responsibility must be very careful to avoid doing harm to our churches. But we who hold leadership responsibility must also face the possibility that we spend a good portion of our energy trying to fend off things that threaten our status and security in our leadership roles. It will be very hard for most of us in church leadership positions to realize that we are guilty of contributing to the church's malnourished condition. We may think that we are protecting the organized life of the church when we are actually protecting ourselves at the expense of the church's decline. We who are now in leadership roles, both laity and clergy, are in great danger of betraying Jesus Christ.

It is ironic to know that we who are charged with responsibility to be leaders in the mainstream church may become so protective of our malnourished charge that we might do our churches lasting harm. We may become so sensitive to outside challenges to our status that we will fight off all intrusions into our bailiwick. Our loyalty and devotion to our churches and our historic ministries may become the greatest hindrance to the church that we cherish. All of us know of overprotective parents and the damage that they inflict on their children's growth. Over-protective leadership is marked by its high sensitivity to external threats. An example of our high sensitivity is shown when a film or television program portrays Jesus or some aspect of Christian faith and tradition in an untraditional light; or when a traditional doctrine of our theology is declared invalid by some prominent person who has some influence with public opinion; or when the Internal Revenue Service rules that clergy are subject to a tax paid by other citizens. Such things arouse our defense mechanisms in a hurry.

The more tightly the doctrines of the church are held, the higher the sensitivity to outside threats of disruption to those doctrines will be. For this reason, among others, the Roman Catholic leaders tend to be more on guard against disruptive outside influences than Protestant leaders usually are. But when it comes to disruptive calls for change made by dissident groups within their organizations, Protestant and Catholic leaders act in the same way. They huddle in caution and try to put a stop to dissention. I know this from personal experience, for I have done my share of trying to quench fires of dissention which threatened to weaken my leadership status. That is to say that as a pastor and church bureaucrat, I tried to keep my job! I have not yet been fired because I gave high priority to avoiding being fired. I tried to be adroit in protecting my flanks. All leaders do this, and the question of whether we help or hinder the church when we do this is a very hard question for some to answer.

A PROPOSAL: HERMENEUTIC CONVERSATIONS

The substance of my proposal is to enlist all of us, clergy and lay leaders alike, in the spiritual art of what I will call *hermeneutic conversation*. At this point, I wish to make only a preliminary excursion into a discussion of what this implies or calls for. In the next chapter I will continue the discussion of what I mean by hermeneutic conversation, and I will go more deeply into its ramifications for our needed revitalization.

It is enough at this point to say that hermeneutic conversation is the kind of conversation that seeks to understand what the other person is thinking while the other person gives us a chance to make clear what we are thinking. Hermeneutic is an excellent word which says two things at the same time: explanation and interpretation. The Greeks used the word first to describe how Hermes, the messenger god, kept the other gods informed. Its most popular use is in theological schools where it is used to talk about the art of making the Bible understandable.

The idea of developing a mainstream Protestant church gifted with the art of hermeneutic conversation from bottom to top, small children to senior citizens, is preposterous. It runs contrary to the traditional pattern of the stern preacher in a high pulpit telling the flock what it should believe. It contradicts the idea of drilling little children on their catechism. It opposes the desire on the part of many lay people to have a father or mother figure at the head of the congregation, telling them what to believe. To make matters worse, some lay leaders have become as authoritative as generals themselves after a few years of practice.

The art of listening to others until we know what they really think is a very rare art. One good thing about our clergy trained in non-directive counseling is that many of them have had some practice in the art. Not many of us are good at practicing it in conversation.

This idea of hermeneutic conversational style in our churches is even more complicated than leveling out the playing field of pastors and laity. I have mentioned the bad results that we have gotten out of a non-directive clergy and the non-directional church. An emphasis on hermeneutic conversation could be taken to mean that everyone in the church is of equal authority on all subjects. It may be true that all people have the equal right and responsibility to express an opinion, but not all opinions are equally valid. Every pastor must know a few people whose opinions on certain subjects are worth more consideration than hers or his.

Not only do we have highly educated people in our ranks who know more in their own fields of subject matter than the clergy will ever know, but we also have something else that is of even more importance. Every one of the members of a mainstream Protestant church knows more about herself or himself than anyone else will ever know. Each person is the final authority on what may be central to his or her life. Many people have personal beliefs that are tattered, torn, tired, and more of a bother than they are worth. Others are very sure of everything. Many feel guilty about their unbelief or disbelief, and they keep their unhappy secrets to themselves. We might never be able to classify the array of personality configurations in even the smallest church. But we can be very certain that people want to be understood, and that they also want to understand at least a few other people. To be a relatively normal human being is to be a soul yearning for faithful companionship. We find our most rewarding companionship in the company of human beings who try to understand us while we try to understand them. This means that we share our doubts with one another as readily as we share our beliefs. In this company of mutuality we may often find our lives connected to purposes that enchant existence with great meaning.

Unfortunately, we cannot achieve this companionship with others or invest our lives in vital purposes unless we have achieved substantial accord in a process where sharing doubts and beliefs is experienced in an atmosphere enriched with nourishment provided by new ideas, larger understanding, and more daring reaches of belief. In short, we find our mutuality in a religion that helps us to make sense out of life in company with others. Twenty centuries of Christian church experience demonstrate this.

One of the most interesting lay persons I have ever known is a medicinal chemist who has had much to do with the development of important drugs in everyday use. He became interested in New Testament literature as a hobby, and within a few years he owned a considerable library. He moved to another city and went from one mainstream church to another, trying to find one where beliefs were expressed in language that he could accept in some measure. He needed the fellowship of kindred minds. Finally, he joined a church and accepted a position teaching an adult class. He was distressed by the published materials that the church bought from its denominational press for use in its adult classes. His letter was an appeal for help: "How do we move away from the stereotypes so firmly embedded in the educational materials fed to us? I cannot accept them. Some others can, but many have my trouble."

My reply to him was in terms of establishing the kind of exchange I am here calling the hermeneutic conversation: "Get the people to really open up for you their true belief systems." A few years later he told me that it took weeks to get people to come out into the open to talk about what they had once believed but no longer accepted. It took even longer for those who accepted what was printed in the materials to accept without anxiety the people in the class who were rejecting almost everything. With careful guidance and a lot of stimulation from the leader, they gradually developed the spiritual ability to explain what they meant by the words they used. What they found was a surprising amount of disbelief or unbelief in many of the traditional doctrines about prayer, death, resurrection, heaven, hell, and all of the rest of the very long list.

The hermeneutic conversation properly developed in the mainstream Protestant churches would expose an enormous field of unbelief or disbelief. But the people in our churches, clergy and laity alike, seem incapable at the present time of this high quality of conversation. Why are we so incapable? Because we have always put our emphasis on the importance of belief and have developed the habit of telling people what they must or should believe. This process of being told what we should believe about God, Jesus, and all the rest begins for many Christians at an age when they can barely talk. Mainstream Protestantism has developed on the foundation of the basic proposition that we are to believe what we are taught to believe. We do not have to search long to find sincere mainstream Protestants who are grounded firmly in the indoctrination of children and youth.

We have not left room for an open discussion of beliefs that have eroded. We have even taken great pains to avoid any appearance that traditional beliefs and symbols could erode.

There is an unmentioned assumption, or hope, that the Holy Church of Jesus Christ will be allowed to avoid revolutionary changes in its belief system.

Hermeneutic conversation accepts and honors the human mind, and it welcomes serious talk and candid writing. There is an assumption in this acceptance that the human mind needs conversation to clarify the way it understands life. There is also the assumption that language flowing back and forth between two or more people can yield great values when the people engaged in discourse do not pretend to hold beliefs that are not truly held. Hermeneutic conversation is achieved when minds share without deceit, cunning, or guile of any kind. When we share what we firmly know in our minds and hearts, we have done only half of what we must do in hermeneutic conversation. The other half is done when we hear what another strives to say and when we do our part to comprehend even beyond the words we hear.

THINKING CHRISTIANS

The malnourished mainstream Protestant church is literally filled with people who have decided to think for themselves, but who find that they cannot think for themselves as they had thought that they might. In some cases, these people have made a small venture into thinking for themselves and have been frightened back into the safety of an orthodoxy that they can pretend to believe even though they do not believe it. Or, in the absence of opportunities to share their gnawing disbeliefs with others in their church, they may turn to a pseudo-religious group where the more they deny what they once believed, the more popular their voices become. Nevertheless, by the tens of thousands they discover this is not what they wanted either.

Today our mainstream Protestant churches are composed of people who have been encouraged to think for themselves in public schools and institutions of advanced learning. But they have not been taught how to think about the Christian religion in terms of the theological and biblical advances that have taken place in this century and continue to take place in our theological schools. Though there is not consensus in these schools, we would all benefit from hermeneutic conversations about major movements taking place now. Lacking this nurture for our thinking processes, we have become a malnourished reformation composed of believing unbelievers and unbelieving believers. The believing unbelievers recite the creeds, sing the hymns, and listen to the sermons in suffering tolerance. On the other hand, the unbelieving believers do not believe the prevailing teaching or preaching, but they stay in their churches because they still hope against hope that things will change for the better.

REAL CONVERSATIONS

The hermeneutic conversation, skillfully exercised, would uncover the real extent of these conditions. But there is no ability to do this sort of thing because we are not trained by our experiences in life to think of conversations in which the central purpose is to make sure that we understand others and that they understand us. It is a far cry from the mainstream Protestant church to the American automobile industry, but an example from this industry illuminates the nature of our task in learning how to nurture our malnourished church.

When the American auto manufacturers rather suddenly discovered that they had serious competition from Japanese manufacturers, they acted, at first, as if they did not believe what was happening. After several years of international market losses, the Americans realized that they were not the top of the heap as they had always been. Americans were buying Japanese cars, and one poll after another reported that Americans were doing so because the Japanese manufacturers were producing a better automobile.

It took several years for American manufacturers to learn that there was one basic difference in their management practices and those of the Japanese. The Japanese managers listened to the workers on the factory floor, ate with the workers, parked their cars in the same lots as the workers, and dressed in clothing not much different from that worn by the assembly line workers. In American manufacturing there has long been an adversary relationship between managers and workers. It has proven to be extremely difficult to change this pattern. Such change would require that managers learn how to listen to workers on the assembly line and that workers on the factory floor learn how to listen with understanding and to share what they know with accuracy.

This suggests how difficult it will be for us to learn how to carry out a hermeneutic conversation. It means that each of us will go all the way to the bottom of our deepest concerns and will learn how to face things together. Our mainstream churches must open up the hidden doubts of the laity and clergy and, at the same time, must find ways to encourage the people to speak out in candor about their true beliefs and fearful doubts. Doing this will require the complete renovation of our educational materials for the earliest ages to the oldest among us. It will require the "opening up" of all of our cherished doctrines in ways that encourage members and leaders on every level to engage freely in doubting without fear of ridicule or reprisal. It will honor Tennyson's observation that,

> There lives more faith in honest doubt,
> Believe me, than in half the creeds.[2]

Many people will think that I am putting too much emphasis on doubting. My experience proves to me that opening up doubt is a sure way to new faith. When I was appointed to Memorial United Methodist Church in White Plains, New York, I was deeply depressed by the quality of adult education in the church. On my first Sunday morning there, I walked along the beautiful corridor that led to the large and attractive rooms where adult classes were meeting. There were four well-filled rooms. I tactfully told the teachers that I wanted to visit each class, in turn, and to sit on the back row to listen. I sat in each class and listened to a teacher do all of the talking while the people sat passively and listened. This same sort of thing takes place every Sunday all across America. It was too terrible to endure, so I decided to be as tactful as I could in offering something else.

I felt sure that there were many in our membership who would appreciate a different approach to the Christian faith. But I already knew that this was touchy territory. I met with the adult leaders and told them that I thought it would be a good thing to begin another group which would discuss contemporary issues and theology. I told them that I wanted to lead the group, and they were delighted at this new pastoral interest in teaching a class. They had not had a pastor who was willing to add a Sunday morning class to his or her schedule. I also told them that I hoped it would be a class entirely composed of people not already in one of the existing four classes. This seemed to reassure the few who were a little uncertain about having another adult class as competition.

With the way cleared, and with an understanding that I hoped people would stay with their established classes, a discussion group was announced. It would meet to discuss John A. T. Robinson's book *Honest to God,* which had just come out in America. The book was being hailed by some critics and condemned by others for its adoption of Bultmann's theology and his views about demythologizing the New Testament. Within a few weeks, this discussion group included about seventy-five persons. Many persons were newly brought by church members who had not been attending either of the four classes.

This was a no-holds barred discussion group, and it became known around the church as "the atheists group." When I heard the label, I tried to show no reaction. The name stuck. After finishing Robinson's book, we turned to the Bible and put emphasis on understanding it as literature. It was my job to pass along to the group, in condensed form, recent scholarship about the work before us. Interest remained high. Every Christian doctrine was discussed, and doubts were expressed as freely as beliefs. We had the usual professional doubters, but they were respected and accepted. They contributed much to the growth of beliefs in the group.

Twenty-five years after that class was begun, it is still remembered as a vital point in the life of that church, and today's leadership has its roots in the deepening of belief that resulted from the opening up of our mutual doubts and deep beliefs. We had engaged in hermeneutic conversations on a level of mutuality. Everyone there knew that I had more theological and biblical training than anyone else. But there were others whose competence in their own fields was recognized as having superior value for our discussions. Included were a psychiatrist, a book editor, musicians, computer programmers, women dedicated to raising children, and people from other walks of life. Their special competence increased the validity of our hermeneutical conversations on Sunday mornings.

There was a basic reason why I could believe that opening up doubts in the congregation would be a sure way to make ventures in the development of faith. My first church as a pastor was a tiny congregation of people struggling for economic survival on the open prairie of southeastern Colorado. They had not had a pastor for nine years. I had just graduated from college and was debating the choice of vocation. Theological school was a future possibility. Neighbors were separated by miles of prairie, which was planted to grow wheat but was barren eight months of the year. We were soon to be the Dust Bowl.

I felt a need to know something about the history of philosophy. Will Durant's *Story of Philosophy* was among the books in the box that I had brought to our little prairie shanty. Copies could be bought for a dollar. I bought a dozen copies on credit and announced the beginning of a Wednesday night discussion group. The room in our home that we called "the parlor" was our meeting place. Ten people came. Our lighting fixture was a hissing Coleman lantern. We discussed the philosophers, but we discussed even more God, prayer, hell, heaven, suicide, and every topic of interest to anyone in the group. We shared our doubts and our beliefs. One man wore his sombrero and chewed tobacco throughout the entire evening. He loved Schopenhauer. This man said that his daughter had brought a dictionary into their dugout home and he had to look up a lot of words. I told him that I had the same problem with Schopenhauer.

I owe to that little discussion group in the Stonington "parsonage" a lifelong debt that I can never repay. Those wonderful people of unsurpassed courage and gentleness taught me to respect the human mind and its doubts and to prize the human mind for its insatiable hunger to know more about the meaning of our lives together. Today I know that we achieved a high quality of hermeneutic conversation. I was not to hear the word *hermeneutic* for many years, but now I know what happened within our circle.

The average mainstream Protestant congregation in America has about two hundred members. Many pastors serve more than one congregation. All of these pastors are kept busy and work long hours in dedication to the service of families and individuals. Any choice to spend time in any particular way is a hard choice, and all pastors wish that they had just a little more time for reading and reflection. All pastors wish they could afford to buy the books that they feel they should read.

The wonderful people in my first appointment taught me without intending to do so. They taught me that my own intellectual and spiritual welfare depended on holding herme- neutic conversations with them. There was not a single college graduate in the group, but there were honest human beings with a hunger to open up their own minds and hearts—once they were convinced that their pastor was not holding anything back from them. We met as earnest seekers after knowledge, and it was our need to know and understand that brought us together over miles of rough, unpaved roads.

There are many thousand congregations just like that one in Stonington, Colorado. The six other congregations I served were just like my first, in that the minds and hearts of the people were open to hermeneutic conversations about those things that pertain to God and the meaning of human life.

THE PRACTICAL THEOLOGIAN

What comes next? From all parts of the western world we are hearing a new plea: "Let the pastor be our theologian in residence." One of the best examples of this plea is from John de Gruchy, Professor of Christian Studies at Cape Town University in South Africa. Writing from the context of South African apartheid, de Gruchy poses the problems of theology with careful inclusion of warnings against the things that erode the fullness of faith in the community that I am here calling the church organization. He says the pastoral role must meet "our definition of the practical theologian as one who provides leadership and direction for the community of faith."[3]

Throughout the last two decades, our periodicals produced primarily for the clergy have debated what the work pattern of pastors should be. One issue of *The Circuit Rider,* the United Methodist's journal for its clergy, reviewed the question of whether or not there is an impending clergy shortage. One pastor who also serves in his denomination as a secretary of a Board of Ministry wrote: "Much of the current, often justified, lay outcry over clergy incompetence is the result of a system in which too many clergy have been assigned to do too little work. . . . The result is frustration and demoralization for both pastor and congregation."[4] I would change this slightly: most pastors don't do too little work; they do the wrong kind of work.

The malnourished mainstream Protestant church cannot be served without great changes in the quality and work patterns of its key leaders, the pastors. But we make a big mistake if we assume that we can change our existing pastoral leaders without changing our lay leaders on all levels and all of our other leaders, including those at the top and in our theological schools. As a very practical matter, no real change in the work patterns of church leaders, lay and clergy, can possibly come until the leaders at the very top of our leadership caste system see the necessity and change their patterns. Our malnourished church will never be properly nurtured with our existing work patterns in the ministry to the organization.

The labor of hermeneutic conversations calls for creative revolution of the entire communication system within our churches. This revolution must take place in all of our printed materials, audiovisual materials, services of worship, preaching, classroom teaching, and pastoral care. The mainstream Protestants are in a new world where the art of communication among people in hermeneutic conversations will exact new energy from the leadership in a new work pattern.

Unfortunately, our leadership is incapable of the task imposed upon it without extreme changes in the ways that we use our minds and employ our time. Is such an extreme shift possible? I believe it is. There is enough frustration in our leadership ranks right now to make a promising change welcome.

CHAPTER
IV

THE PARALYSIS OF MAINSTREAM LEADERSHIP

THE PROTESTANT CASTE SYSTEM

The leadership of mainstream Protestant churches is arranged into five castes or layers. At the top in prestige and authority are the bishops or their equivalents. Some denominations are allergic to the title of bishop for good reasons of their own. But these denominations have general superintendents, stated clerks, or some other officials who do what bishops are supposed to do.

Next to the top are the bureaucrats who have executive responsibility for the denominational boards and agencies. Although these leaders may sometimes come from the laity, they are more often from the ranks of the clergy. They have more power, in some respects, than the bishops because they have charge of money and programs to use it. The bishops cultivate the bureaucrats' favor most of the time. To be a good bureaucrat, one must know the caste system and have a good relationship with people in the other castes. Bishops and bureaucrats in the mainstream church have a symbiotic relationship. This may provoke some unhappiness in other castes where a few envy their power which is more apparent than real.

The middle caste in the leadership ranks is composed of the pastors. They are supposed to be totally dedicated to the pastoral task and to have no ambition for being either a bureaucrat or a bishop. To openly declare such an ambition is a sure way of guaranteeing that one will continue to be a pastor. There have been a few instances when pastors have declined election to the office of bishop. There are more instances where pastors have declined to serve in the bureaucratic caste, but even these incidents attract some attention. However, nobody knows better than the bishops and bureaucrats that the most important of all leadership roles is that of the pastor in the local church.

The leadership caste underneath the pastoral rank is composed of both laity and clergy and is therefore quite confusing in some ways. This is the caste that runs the regional structures which are fondly called "the judicatories." These are the annual conferences, synods, presbyteries, and so forth. Leadership in this caste has much more change in its membership because there are usually limited terms for those who hold office. However, this statement can be misleading because the churches have their lifetime career people who move from one office to another when a term in one office expires. Sometimes these people are referred to as "church politicians"—but seldom in a derogatory tone. Without the useful services of such people, the church would be less effective than it is.

The bottom of the caste system is the leadership in the local church. It must not be understood that this caste is less important because they are on the bottom of the leadership group. This is the foundational caste composed entirely of the laity. They teach, organize, raise funds, care for the property, and serve the community in many ways. Just as a house must have a good foundation, so must the mainstream Protestant leadership group have a good foundation. The local church is the birthplace of all levels of leadership, and what happens in its life is determinative in all levels of the denomination. It must be emphasized that this bottom of the leadership caste system can either make or break the church. The church lives or dies by how well the pastors and these local church leaders perform their task of nurturing Christian beliefs that eventuate in Christian behavior, which has personal and social significance.

Mainstream Protestant leadership is deployed in a real caste system, although it is a very practical and workable arrangement. When I was in the bureaucratic caste, we had our annual meetings at the same time that the bishops had theirs, but it was axiomatic that we did not meet in the same city. There were certain unwritten rules in our relationships. There are also specific unwritten rules where pastors are concerned. Some things the laity cannot do but pastors can do, such as administer the Lord's Supper or baptize converts.

Less tangible untouchables prevail in the ranks below the pastors, but these untouchables are real. Attending certain official meetings, voting on proposals, making decisions for the group and speaking on their behalf are duties assigned according to the office one holds. All social organizations must have specific arrangements of this kind to preserve order and to perpetuate management.

Finally, some church members never hold an office of any kind. They remain fixed in the caste system on the local church membership level. Although these people may be the treasures of our community, in this discussion they are not considered to be leaders. Because there are so many who are not leaders, we wonder about what kind of person will become a church leader.

THE CHURCH LEADER

Many years ago, Karen Horney, a psychoanalyst and graduate of Union Theological Seminary in New York, said in her book *The Neurotic Personality of Our Time* that people who rise to the top in churches tend to be the kind who run over the people who are meek and mild. She thought that church leaders tend to be more aggressive, egotistical, assertive, and sometimes more laden with hostility toward others than the people who chose "not to run."

No doubt she was right, but only up to a point. She was correct in saying that some of the most ambitious, aggressive, self-assertive people scramble into church leadership roles. People of this personality type can be found throughout any leadership system. I know of no formal study to sort things out, but my impression based on long participation in the leadership ranks causes me to differ with her. A very high proportion of the people in all five castes are there to serve God and other people at some cost to their own convenience, if the cost is not too great.

If we are such high-minded and dedicated people, then why is the church declining under our leadership? I have already offered some explanation of why the mainstream Protestant church is declining. I have argued that its belief systems are not working and that the church is malnourished. But these arguments do not explain why church leaders are failing. It is our job as leaders to see that our organizations' belief systems are nourished. We are supposed to provide, in some practical measure, what our church members need to sustain effectively their faith and their work to convert the world to the life of love. Why are we failing to do what we are supposed to do? Why are we held at bay by forces that we have spawned?

There may be some who will say that only the Holy Spirit can redeem the churches from their decline. I take issue with that view. That kind of declaration makes God totally responsible for what happens in mainstream Protestantism. I believe that the Holy Spirit of God works in the world, but in human affairs the Holy Spirit can work through us only when we use our freedom in a responsible way. This belief is inspired by the biblical story. The church is a social organization dedicated to the work assigned to us by our decisions to be Christians for reasons of our own. If we are not doing well, then the problem is in us, the church's leaders.

This is taking a somewhat narrow view of things. It would sound more elegant to talk about raising the whole rank and file of forty million mainstream Protestants in a national revival. However, such talk is unrealistic. Critical study of social organizations reveals that what happens to any social organization is dependent on whether the leaders can feed energy into the organization in the form of ideas and verbalized goals that the people feel obliged to accept. Mainstream Protestantism will continue to decline until we who are in leadership are moving with great energy and strength to nurture the belief systems and to define significant goals that have the full sanction of our theology and biblical understanding.

THE SYMPTOMS OF OUR PARALYSIS

Why are we not doing what we must do? Why are we paralyzed? The word *paralysis* describes, in a general way, a person who has lost the ability to make voluntary movements. The ability to move voluntarily may be lost through psychological or physiological malfunction. Perhaps a nerve has been damaged or some terrible anxiety is hindering the body's functions, and the paralyzed person is relatively helpless.

Almost everyone has had a bad dream in which terrible things are happening and the ability to run, walk, jump, or cry for help is gone. Some horrifying threat looms over your body, and every limb is frozen by invisible powers that come from nowhere in particular. I have been awakened by dreams in which I felt utterly helpless in the face of disasters so bodiless and undefined that I cannot even give a hint as to what I feared in the dream. But the horror of my paralysis when I wanted so desperately to move was clear enough. I can recall a few times when that kind of nightmare stayed with me into the next morning. I felt its weight.

We who are church leaders have big goals of working toward a better world made fit for God's children to walk in. But our ranks are thinning, our influence is declining, and we cannot work and witness as we had expected. We falter at the foot of molehills; we cannot move mountains. Our paralysis tortures us day and night because we have memories of our fairer days, and our hopes once so fondly held now seem unrealizable.

There are four basic symptoms of our paralysis. *First,* there is an increasing pattern of "power struggling" inside our mainstream churches. We are at war within our own bodies instead of being engaged with the needs of the world for a higher obedience to God. I have already noted the efforts of our insider fundamentalists to gain control of the organizational structures. If that were our only internal power struggle, then we would solve our problem more easily.

The less prominent power struggles take place between boards and agencies. They find it harder than ever to do what they are supposed to do because their goals are increasingly obscure. The eroding belief system affects them all. A board assigned to manage overseas missionary work will be challenged by a board charged with managing the denominational educational work. Or the board assigned responsibility to define social ethics may try to take over work that the educational board is supposed to do.

Too much internal rivalry between boards and agencies of a denomination is a sign of leadership paralysis. It is not extreme to suggest that this unattractive rivalry is something like the unsuccessful efforts of a paralyzed person to open the door and walk out into the world. Everyone wishes it might happen because we want our boards and agencies to spend their money and energies on the main task, which is not to indulge in a quiet internecine conflict. However, paralyzed leaders cannot open the door.

Second, a sure signal of paralysis is when leadership begins to make more and more of ritual, tradition, finery of symbols, and special attractions. It seems there may be some relationship between the increased splendor of vestments in the chancel and the declining power of the sermon as a redeeming and saving word. It would be extreme to say that when heavy pectoral crosses adorn the vestments of the clergy there is a functional decline in passionate dedication to justice, mercy, and good faith, but the ancient prophets took a dim view of too much emphasis on finery. This sounds puritanical, but it isn't. I only point to the symptom of concentrating on things that are not even secondary and making those incidental things the focus of intense concern. In some cases, the opposite of liturgical revival is displayed. This is evident in the pitifully ridiculous efforts of some mainstream leaders to make their church services into poor imitations of show business. This usually includes considerable cuteness with much hugging, kissing, and the singing of trivial ditties. Once I was away from home and invited some friends who belong to no church to attend a Sunday service with me. What took place that Sunday morning still embarrasses my memory. My friends refer to it, somewhat irreverently, as "Sweaty Palm Sunday." They were as anxious and uneasy as I was, but the pastor seemed to be having a wonderful time taking center stage for an hour.

Third, there is a definite symptom of paralyzed leadership when a leader finally believes that small is better. There are pastors who rationalize their membership declines by saying that it is a good thing for their churches to purify their ranks. This attitude does not compliment those who have dropped out.

Of course, an organization can become too large to manage. There are times when structures should be changed in favor of making them manageable. But this is not what the "small is better" argument is saying. The "small is better" argument is a rationalization of leadership failure.

Fourth, and perhaps most striking, is the symptom of working harder and harder at doing the things that no longer bring results. Here is where the top caste is exposed, because it is not at all rare for the top caste to join the bureaucrats in announcing a great program that is imposed with considerable pressure down through the leadership system. The rank and file membership of the organization would be helped by all of this effort if there were new ideas to help them make more sense out of life. They would be helped by fresh theology and new biblical insights, but that isn't in store for them. With their usual loyalty, the membership respond bravely to the trumpet sounds from on high. When the results are meager, they do not complain. The lower echelons in the leadership caste system are just as paralyzed as those who are higher up in the system. They can't even complain aloud.

These urgent calls to work harder at things that do not get results produce an insidious spiritual erosion in the membership ranks. When one adds up all the campaigns, priority calls, and crusades of the past forty years, the mainstream Protestants show no shortage. This symptom of working harder and harder at doing things that do not get results is a sure sign that paralysis is far advanced. This symptom is becoming more pronounced.

Paralyzed leaders are not dead, but they are ineffective. They are not able to do what they are supposed to be able to do, which means that we must go beyond the symptoms to put our finger on the cause of the symptoms. When leaders do not lead, what has caused them to be so incapable?

THE CAUSES OF LEADERSHIP PARALYSIS

In some cases, the ineffective leaders are content with the way things are, and they don't want to be bothered with the hard work required to make changes in their beliefs and working styles. Indifference equals paralysis.

Some leaders had few qualifications in the first place. They may inwardly know that things are not going well, but they are content with the knowledge that the church will remain strong enough to preserve their status and to give them a pension when they retire. This sentiment is along the same line as Madame Pompadour's words to Louis XV after the defeat of the French and Austrian armies by Frederick the Great: "After us the deluge." The number of church leaders who feel this way is probably small, but I know a few who do. However, I have only heard two pastors make such a remark. This attitude is kept under cover.

There are very few contented, complacent, smug mainstream church leaders these days. Our problem is excessive anxiety. This contributes to our paralysis. The more we know about our decline, the more anxious we become. Our anxiety compounds all our other symptoms, and this confuses us. Just as in the case of a medical problem, every time we think we have approached a solution to finding the disease, we discover that we have only found another symptom. Diagnosis of our problem requires self-examination. We mainstream Protestant leaders must face the truth about ourselves and discover why we cannot lead, although we desperately wish that we could. What is wrong with us? This is a most painful question for us to ask ourselves. We may not be able to ask it, and in that case we are lost.

Our leadership paralysis is caused by an infection of the spirit which results in the eventual death of imagination in the life of the leader. Imagination is underrated. Imagination is the work of the mind as it responds to mental notions that may be fleeting and elusive at first. Imagination is the first mental stage of the mind working to capture emerging visions that may be forged into ideas to be tested by critical evaluation.[1] Imagination is the fertile soil in which God's Holy Spirit lures us to take the wings of the dove. It is then up to us to find our own solid Ararat.

It is to the everlasting discredit of the Christian churches that they exert pressures from every direction to stifle imagination. The social organization we call our church is so protective of its ideas, patterns of action, and patterns of thought that it systematically handicaps or punishes imaginative people. The history of the church includes records of the unfortunate things that happen to heretics and innovators.

From a practical standpoint, the mainstream Protestant church must fend off the innumerable crazy notions that emerge with pretensions of seeking the church's welfare. It is true that imagination may produce weird ideas that lead people into serious troubles. Imagination can be very dangerous. So too is electricity a fatal possibility, at times. Imagination, like electricity, must be handled carefully to make it useful. In human affairs, the best way to handle imagination is to involve it in hermeneutic conversation, where it can be tested in the public square.

What, then, must we church leaders do to liberate imagination and allow it to function in our lives as a source of health and vitality? There is a way to do this that has demonstrated its worth. When imagination is confined in suitable arrangements for the testing of its flow, it yields its benefits. In this context we are concerned with the belief system of the mainstream Protestant churches. Ideas originating in imagination are not beliefs. They offer the ingredients that may eventually become beliefs.

The ingredients for the formation of beliefs are formed in the creative channeling of imaginative discourse. In the mainstream Protestant church, this channeling process is in the hermeneutic conversation where theology and the advances in biblical insights are fully invested. Our leadership paralysis is caused by our failure to understand our doubts while, at the same time, we speak as truthfully as we can about our beliefs. We are a paralyzed leadership because we do not realize the severe erosions of belief, nor do we open our lives to the richer and more inspiring beliefs that God holds in store for us.

This leads us to the larger question of whether our paralysis can ever be cured. If our leadership paralysis is not cured, then the mainstream Protestant movement will continue to languish in America and will become a social relic. It will be remembered with fondness and ignored as a contemporary cultural force. Our tragedy will be compounded if our leaders allow their imaginative powers to decline further.

FINDING A CURE

The first step in finding a cure for our paralysis of mind and heart will be the hardest. We will have to admit our needs. This is the same as saying that we must rid ourselves of our denial techniques. We must openly recognize in mainstream Protestant churches that we have a leadership breakdown or failure. We must stop our evasion which often blames external causes for our decline. Our pride in our past must not be allowed to cause us to engage in denial techniques which prevent us from knowing the truth about ourselves. We, the leaders, are what's wrong with mainstream Protestantism today.

This confession of our failure to be true leaders will come hard for all of us up and down the scale of caste relationships. It is so important for us to feel that we are successful. We habitually feel obligated to avoid anything that puts us in the light of being unable to perform our functions. We who have been assigned to act as church leaders are a proud company. It will be a crushing experience to admit that our failure to give full play to imagination and submit to hermeneutic conversations has produced a poverty of belief in our mainstream churches.

We will inevitably be tempted to say, "My beliefs are just fine! If everyone else would just adopt my beliefs, then we could go on together." Most strong leaders feel this way because they must have a strong confidence in their beliefs if they wish to be strong leaders. But what if our belief is contradicted by evidence of some kind that has convinced a number of very competent people? We may still be right, but humility is called for.

One might suppose that a bishop would have more difficulty admitting leadership failure than anyone else. After all, a bishop is supposed to know how to lead by the time that she or he gets to that position in the leadership ranks. When a bishop or general superintendent announces a change of mind on beliefs about God, Jesus, prayer, resurrection, or any other central subject of the Christian religion, there is a public stir. When Bishop John A. T. Robinson of Woolrich published *Honest to God* in 1963, there were two dominant reactions. A few people thought that he was making a substantial contribution to the forwarding of the Christian movement. Most people wondered how a bishop could change his mind so greatly and still hold his office. Some people said he wasn't a Christian because he had departed from the official faith. Bishops do not like this kind of spotlight exposure.

Bishops are not alone in their distaste for public criticism. Most of us shy away from being accused of betraying old beliefs which have gathered a certain quality of honor in our circle of associates. We value consistency for good reasons, but consistency may cause us to stop growing in our intellectual and emotional capacities. By the time we reach adulthood, many, if not most of us, have acquired the habit of avoiding changes in what we say we believe. We push our doubts back and say nothing about them. We may not realize that we are deeply affected by this repression of doubts that are not allowed to surface through our professed beliefs. This repression of honest doubt can paralyze our ability to act because it undermines the beliefs we outwardly profess.

If we assume that of the forty million mainstream Protestants there are about five million in the leadership ranks at any given time, then we have a fair idea of our total target group. It would be a very serious mistake to assume that all of these leaders are eagerly waiting to be cured of a paralysis they do not know they have. Not all of these five million will be responsive, no matter what we try to do.

However, we now have enough restless leaders waiting for a new direction to be encouraged. It is not unrealistic to think that a significant portion of existing leadership can be involved in hermeneutic conversations in theology and biblical studies which will liberate minds and hearts to enjoy wider horizons than we have known in Christian experience.

If we can break through our fears of being criticized for changing our minds, then we will not only understand ourselves better, but we also will love others more. Our capacity to assume the responsibility of courageous leadership in areas of greater service to human need depends in great measure on our ability to overcome old doubts by adopting firmer beliefs.

It would be prudent to assume that in our desire to do something about our leadership we will encounter formidable denial of need. But it will not be more formidable on the top level than it is on the bottom. The entire leadership system is set in concrete, and there are two major reasons for this.

First, most of the people in the leadership ranks believe that the church is indestructible and has its own survival powers, regardless of how badly they do their jobs. This view has liturgical reinforcements. All of us have recited prayers about the Church that will triumph, will last to the "end of time," and will have the everlasting power of God to ensure its victory. When we have offered these prayers and sung these hymns in all sincerity, it has seldom dawned on us that, while this may be true of the Church (with a capital *C*), it is not necessarily true of the congregation or group of congregations we have been charged to lead. All of us in the leadership castes have been infected with a theological notion of guaranteed success.

We know what overconfidence has done to undermine the effectiveness of basketball teams, merchants, doctors, kings, and parents. Having no confidence at all is destructive, but having too much confidence can result in failing to do what is essential. We mainstream leaders were riding high until of late, and we have not yet fully realized how much we have been taking for granted. There are still thousands of thriving mainstream local churches in America today. Most of the leaders of these thriving churches are noticing the first signals of decline. These fortunate leaders will do well to take these first signals seriously and to begin now to nurture the failing belief systems of the entire membership body.

The second element that holds us in fixed position is our love of our church. We do not want to harm it in any way. Leaders love their organization, and this makes them blind to "the follies they themselves commit." In the *Merchant of Venice,* the potential follies that Portia has in mind are the little mistakes that undermine the whole structure of an enterprise.

In our love for the church we have acquired the collective ability to shield the members from the new knowledge about our world and the Bible. We have been doing this because we fear that this knowledge will undermine the faith of our people, and we know—or think that we know—what this will mean. We have a genuine concern for the health and welfare of persons. We know how devastating our influence is when it undermines the only beliefs people have left. We have failed to use our imaginations to create new expressions of belief that will mean even more to our people in our contemporary flux.

In our caution to avoid destroying the beliefs of our people, we have been failing to nurture them to higher, richer, more solidly founded beliefs. Because we have not developed the art of hermeneutic discourse, we have not cultivated the freedom of our church members to enjoy the pleasure of imagination and the enrichment of their minds. We have allowed our people to languish. Our paralysis of leadership results in a damaging caution that impoverishes belief. We have let the church settle into stagnation.

It would be unfair and cynical to say that we have been doing this to save our jobs. Almost all local church leaders serve their churches on a volunteer basis at a personal cost of money and time. They are true and honest believers. In the leadership castes where people are paid to do a job, there are few instances where those people could not step right out of the church into jobs paying twice as much money. I could never agree with the cynical view that we have been defending our jobs when we have tried to shelter our own people from new truths that upset their old beliefs. There is something else that is operative in this conflict of the new and old.

Ask any pastor in any of the mainstream Protestant churches why he or she is going so slow in introducing new ideas in theology or new theories about the Bible. Some will insist that nothing is being held from their members. However, I have found that if the conversation goes on long enough, even these pastors will say, "I am going as fast as the situation permits." Most pastors will come right out and say, "I am not going to destroy the faith of my members."

When this book was in an early stage of development, I asked the publisher to secure some reactions from critical readers whose names would remain unknown to me. One of the responses came from a pastor whose tone was somewhat heated. The pastor wrote:

> There is little that is new here, and what is missing is prescriptive help for working pastors who want to base their preaching and ministry on a sound theology pertinent to contemporary life. These pastors do not want to fall prey to the forces of fundamentalism, rationalism, greed, or the psychologizing of religion that Carothers identifies. *Some of us have attempted to do just what he is calling for with the result that we have been stung by harsh criticism and left dangling with little support in our efforts to offer an authentic understanding of the Christian faith for people in the post modern world.* (emphasis added)

I feel identified with this pastor. These comments confirmed my deep conviction that my analysis is on target, and they buttressed my conviction that I know what we must do to move forward.

This discerning pastor knows that we must go forward in leading our mainstream Protestant churches into a new belief system where theology sustains a more inclusive ethic and has the support of new biblical scholarship. This pastor laments what happened when he or she tried! He or she was "stung by harsh criticism and left dangling with little support." This describes a real problem. I cannot avoid thinking that it is quite common for pastors to have similar experiences. If so, it means that we are a very long way from being prepared throughout mainstream Protestantism for the kind of hermeneutic conversations we must learn to hold on a sustained basis.

This issue has troubled me deeply for many years because one pastor after another has told me, "I do not wish to disturb my people with ideas that upset them." I have been told this in almost the same breath that the pastor told me how widely his or her own beliefs differed from those prevailing in the congregation. I am convinced that we cannot hope to revitalize the belief systems and deal constructively with the needs of our malnourished church without opening up constructive ways of being truthful. I have no interest in using new data to tear down faith or disrupt the church, but new developments in theology and biblical studies can be shared in ways that enrich life.

All of us in leadership roles know that the risks involved in dealing with our belief system are serious. We are something like a person who has an artery seriously blocked with cholesterol. If we do nothing, then we are at risk; if we submit to treatment, then we are also at risk. A person who must decide whether or not to run the risk of heart surgery deserves our sympathy. If a parent is required to decide for a beloved child whether or not to run the risk, then the stress of deciding is very great. We who are mainstream Protestant leaders love our church. We may be mistakenly parental in our love. This is one of our more severe hindrances in facing our paralysis of mind and will. Our love for our church becomes a form of denial that requires curative actions.

We must act before it is too late. Mainstream Protestantism does not dare risk continuing what is now being preached and taught. We who are responsible for taking the lead must quit our rationalizing and accept the realities of our predicament. But we must not cripple our church while we are trying to move into the new era.

TAKING THE CURE

Let us now take a look at one leadership group in the mainstream Protestant churches that I have not mentioned: our theological school faculties. My reason for putting them outside the leadership caste system is not a happy one: they have given up on us and we have given up on them.

Most of the two hundred accredited schools in the American Association of Theological Schools have denominational roots, although a few were started on an ecumenical basis. In practice they are generally indifferent to denominationalism. Most schools no longer build their faculties according to the teacher's denominational affiliation. Following World War II these theological schools became the best in the world. Many of them have interlocked with great universities, and their qualified graduates earn degrees by benefiting from great libraries and teachers who are keeping abreast of the advances in theology and biblical studies. It is too often the case that the best students graduate and choose to teach, avoiding the pastoral ministry. Colleges all across the continent find that their students are demanding better courses in religion and biblical studies. So the colleges attract these new scholars into their faculties.

Almost all of these schools are uneasily aware that things are not going well in the churches. Most of them have responded by establishing courses on parish ministry and by assigning faculty members to guide students who hold pastoral assignments. However, there is no real relationship where new knowledge flows back and forth between the theological schools and all levels in our leadership system. I put the emphasis on "back and forth" and "all levels of leadership" because I am under no illusions that our theological schools hold the secret cure for our leadership paralysis.

Indeed, it is quite possible that there is a considerable paralysis of some kind affecting our theological schools, because we have had no signal efforts on their part to come out of their protected halls to run the risks of trying to save mainstream Protestantism from its malnourished condition. Some of the faculty see the condition that we are in, and some of them write about it. But even the most concerned among the faculty members have no effective way to become a part of real interchange with bishops, bureaucrats, pastors, judicatory leaders, and local church leaders. For all practical purposes, our theological schools and their faculties are insulated from our churches, and as a result our churches do not receive a sustained flow of developments in theology and biblical studies.

The breakdown of vital relationships between churches and theological schools is not the fault of anyone. The burden of so much new knowledge in theology and biblical studies is too much for the church leaders to handle without changing their work habits. Theological faculties have the time required for careful study, whereas church leaders are fully occupied with other things. Although the pastoral office was once identified with scholarship, it is now mainly given to church administration. Most pastors have never been trained to do both administration and studying every day of the week.

There is an added difficulty. Pastors soon discover that church members know less than they do about the Christian religion and the Christian way of life. Pastors quickly discover that they can get along with what they have, and so they do. Many theological school graduates have expected to find their church members much more intellectually alive than they turn out to be. Even the recent graduates of liberal arts colleges know next to nothing about history, sociology, and other fields associated with the traditional humanities. In particular, most college graduates are religiously illiterate, but this secular learning hasn't blotted out their religious needs. Lacking a more convincing basis for religious belief, many of them are easy targets for television's religion hucksters. America has become a wasteland of superstitious intellectuals. Malnourishment of beliefs doesn't kill the appetite for believing.

Well-educated people join those less educated in one thing: they gradually come to think of their world in terms defined by the mass media. The mass media includes television, radio, newspapers, magazines, popular books, and that plethora of floating images of the mind that accumulate in locker-room conversations or exchanges at the water fountain in the factory. The new images of our world and the meaning of human life are hammering at our traditional belief system in all of the churches. We mainstream Protestant leaders are failing to understand the force of this impact from the outside. We mainstream Protestants are not serving the American imagination. The American imagination must be stirred by new Christian visions of what a decent life and a decent society can offer.

Tragically, too many of us feel that we are finished with our theological and biblical education because we already know more than our church members do. Edward Farley, professor of theology at Vanderbilt Divinity School, laments that while theological schools prepare students to recognize the need to interpret the world and Scripture in more enlightened ways, these students go into their churches and complacently allow their church members to remain at a literalist level in their religious understanding.[2] This destroys the integrity of the pastor and leaves the church member to wallow in ignorance.

The depth of the problem is further probed by L. Gregory Jones of Loyola College in Maryland. He takes the "most American" church as an example:

> In The United Methodist Church we often separate people into two groups, the laity and clergy, and the laity often express their sense that the clergy don't take seriously their vocation to think theologically. Moreover, The United Methodist Church has not been sure what to do with theologians. Beyond being somewhat grateful to them, the church is on the one hand unsure whether theologians should be ordained and on the other hand suspicious that they are too far removed and abstracted from the church and the church's mission.[3]

Professor Jones, a professor of theology in a church college, calls for an emphasis on the teaching vocation of bishops and their equivalents, pastors, and lay people who choose to make a special vocation of theological and biblical teaching.

It will take a radical series of steps to cure our leadership paralysis once we recognize our need to be cured, and I do not assume that we will recognize our need for a cure without some real shock. This shock might come from an increase in the rate of our membership loss. The 1989 statistics from The United

Methodist Church show an increased rate of decline in spite of the fact that some very optimistic leaders had set the goal of a doubled membership by that year. Other mainstream statistics are the same or worse. The necessary shock into action may be very near.

SWALLOWING THE CURE

In listing the five castes in our mainstream church leadership systems, I did not include our theological school faculties; however, basic to our cure is the development of robust hermeneutic conversations with these faculties. Some of these faculty members are Jews or representatives of Asian religions. I am convinced that our cure involves them because it requires a major movement in the ways that our imaginations are serving our basic need to make sense out of our world.

My proposal brings the theological faculties into the leadership system in ways that have not been used before now. Not for one minute do I think that our salvation is waiting for us in our theological schools. There are tangible reasons why the churches do not quite know what to do about their theological school faculties. The most tangible reason is that most scholars cannot be understood by the rest of us until we corner one of them in a coffee shop for a couple of hours.

However, there are good reasons for this situation. In almost every case, we who are now leaders graduated without taking a single course in some fields. It is possible for a pastor to have a great scholastic record and to graduate at the top of the theological school class having had only one or two courses on the Bible. I will not dwell on this unfortunate circumstance because I recognize that it is impossible for anyone to be a specialist these days in everything that pertains to a vocation.

My proposal looks toward the fusion of our theological faculties into our leadership system in a way that allows beliefs to be infused with imagination that has been subjected to academic disciplines. I do not have in mind the handing down of theology and biblical knowledge by a superior priesthood of the very

93

learned. I do have in mind the effective way that academic disciplines can whip imagination into convincing beliefs.

When we bring a church leader into a hermeneutic conversation with a theological or biblical scholar, we put two opinionated personalities into small space. If there are twenty people of this kind in the room, then there are twenty opinionated personalities. I have noted the impossibility of dialogue between the fundamentalist faction and the establishment leaders in The United Methodist Church. Adding theological school faculty to this combination provides a situation that is difficult for everyone involved. We simply do not know how to talk *with* one another. We only know how to *tell* one another what the truth is. We are habituated to be proclaimers, not to be listeners who really understand. Teachers, preachers, and officials have much in common that makes true hermeneutical discourse unlikely, unless they change their ways of relating to one another. This requires a structured, deliberate approach.

The Cure

My proposal begins with a carefully planned program of bringing the bishops, or their equivalents, and board executives into hermeneutic conversations with our theological school faculties. We should begin with leaders in these castes because of practical considerations: 1) they hold special leadership roles, 2) most of them have been out of theological schools longer than most of the pastors, and 3) we need a very visible demonstration of their willingness to be involved in leading the whole church into the program.

I propose that July and August be considered as special months in which our theological schools open their facilities for a one-month session involving bishops, or their equivalents, board executives, and theological faculties. The church leaders as well as theological faculties should be broadly represented so that the special month becomes a truly ecumenical gathering.

This should be done for at least two consecutive years. Let every theological school make all of its facilities available during this month, and let each denomination give top priority to having its leaders present.

Intersperse the people on the campus by using a system that brings everyone into the discussion groups on the same level. Limit the size of these groups to about twenty persons. Provide for a rotating leadership of the group to insure collegiality.

No group can have an effective hermeneutic conversation unless it has a topic to discuss. This means that a good paper written on a chosen topic must be circulated before the group assembles. Any church leader can list about thirty topics in two minutes.

There will be strong temptation to avoid the most urgent topics, and this means that these topics should be tackled first. I am convinced these most urgent topics must include the immaculate conception and virgin birth of Jesus, the miracles, the Second Coming, physical resurrection of Jesus, and immortality. Also, how we think of the Bible as "the Word of God," prayer, worship, God's power, sin, and salvation.

For an entire month, let the top leadership castes and the faculties share their doubts and their beliefs. They should come to a deep understanding of how they think and what they truly and honestly believe and doubt. That is the only goal of a hermeneutic conversation.

But this goal is not what these strong-minded people usually seek in a group relationship. It is our habit as church leaders and faculty members to impose a view and win consent to that view. We are habitually true believers to the core. This true-believing streak can come out with great force and often seems to have the force of hostility behind it. Recently I attended a service of worship led by a friend who is very fundamentalistic. He was using the Bible in a way he knows to be a contradiction of scholarship even in some fundamentalist circles. We had discussed the point, and he knew where I stood on it. Looking directly at me he said, "I don't care what the scholars say. I am in this pulpit. I know what I believe, and it is true." I must admit that I felt the force of his belief, but I also vowed to absorb the force and to respond hermeneutically when the opportunity came. It is likely that frequent occasions of heated exchange of a similar kind will take place when top leadership castes meet with faculty members. True hermeneutic conversation is never easy. Once a couple of summer months have been spent in high-level conversations in which doubts and beliefs are shared, we mainstream Protestants will then be ready to make important moves through all the other castes in our leadership system. The way all of our mainstream Protestant churches function is about the same. The top castes must often demonstrate their readiness to move ahead before the other castes feel convinced that they are headed in the right direction. This does not really mean that these churches are top-directed. It does mean that there is a surprising amount of mutual respect between the leadership castes—up and down or down and up, as one may choose to think of the relationship.

With this proposal, I am simply being practical. It would be too much to try to involve all leaders at first. We must begin somewhere, and it seems best to begin with those who have been selected to be leaders on a specified level.

Making It Happen

It will be very hard to convince church leaders and theological faculties that this proposal is worth the time and expense. My personal experience indicates that most things that happen in a denomination have their beginning in the mind of a solitary person who then gets a few others involved. Together they work out certain specific steps to take. These steps are determined by all of the numerous practical considerations that abound to prevent anything new from ever developing. The weight of organizational immobility cannot be exaggerated.

It will be extremely difficult to convince these leaders and faculty members that the summer months of July and August be set apart for the healing of leadership paralysis in mainstream Protestantism. Even those theological schools that have successful summer schools will wonder how they can ever accommodate another invasion of the summer interval—a time for research, writing, and recreation.

The people in the church leadership castes also have their summer habits. Many church leaders attend meetings all summer long, some of which are held on other continents or in lovely retreat centers. Giving a whole month to living on a theological school campus, sleeping in a dormitory, eating institutional food, and risking nights without air conditioning seems like a huge sacrifice.

Even worse, imagine sitting quietly in a group to hear some person describe a personal belief or doubt that one does not share and for which one has limited tolerance. What could be more dreadful than listening to someone indulge in sentimentality, irrationality, and lazy ignorance? Hermeneutic conversation does not come free. One must learn how to suffer fools gladly, for each of us may be the fool if given enough time. To convince leaders that this program is essential, we must face real hurdles and somehow manage to get over them.

Although the relationship between the two top castes (bishops, their equivalents, and bureaucrats) is functionally cordial, it must be recognized that the top caste may have certain streaky feelings of superiority and the bureaucrats may shelter unconscious hostility toward their organizational superiors. We are dealing with strong personalities.

It is possible that a few faculty members may feel separated from the church leaders by the intricate nature of these leaders' detailed knowledge. Only a few can be expected to know very much about the distinctive skills that these church functionaries must have in order to be where they are in the organization. Most faculty members have been in the relative freedom of the academic environment long enough to have forgotten how adroit a bishop or bureaucrat must be to survive organizational tides which ebb and flow with very tricky currents. Mutual respect must be earned, but it will come in due course of time in true hermeneutical conversation.

The ultimate achievement in hermeneutic conversation is reached when a top church leader or a distinguished theologian can respond patiently as one is often required to do in a Vermont town meeting. Vermonters usually have a word of wisdom for all moments of great need. A Vermonter may listen to an incoherent speaker in Town Meeting and then arise to remark, "I hear what you say, but I don't know what you mean." This remark is a courteous request for deeper unfolding of real intentions. It asks for some hermeneutical exchange on a subject of real importance.

The agenda for these hermeneutical conversations should not be terribly difficult. I have noted the subjects that already divide us in subtle ways that result in our malnourished churches. We need to unfold our affirmative declarations that take us beyond fundamentalism so that we no longer sound like the fundamentalists. We must enter into new ways of talking to one another about our experience of God so that we may know God in the immediate immanence of ordinary things.

Through the exchanges of hermeneutic conversations we should discover the ways that our materialism continues to keep the poor people in their poverty. Hermeneutic conversations on this matter will require church leaders and most theological faculty members to explore disciplines in sociology and economics, and to discover how such disciplines must be linked to any full preaching of God's presence in our world now. This will be a fearsome venture for thousands among us who will have the undefined anxiety that they are abandoning a precious treasure. It takes courage to pick up our bed and walk. There is real danger that we will refuse to exchange our weakening estate for a stronger vitality.

Recovery from our leadership paralysis will require that after two summers have been given by the top leadership castes to the development of real hermeneutic conversations on the matters of mainstream Protestant belief, we will then involve all of our other levels in the same depth until we have generated a new church. Within the organizational life of this new church it will be as natural as breathing to entertain new theological concepts and new biblical discoveries, and to share with one another our doubts as easily as we share our beliefs.

With a vital belief system of this flexible kind in place, we can then be aware of the immediate immanence of God in ordinary occasions, and we will be able to sustain a more inclusive ethic. Our church organization will be healthy because a cured leadership will be feeding it with new ideas that can be expressed in more venturesome and creative acts of love. We can minister to American culture as we should be ministering now.

In the short chapters that follow, I will offer what I believe to be some fundamental considerations that will come up in hermeneutic conversations. If I am proved wrong in my estimates, I feel sure that something better will emerge, and I look forward to sharing in it.

CHAPTER
V

HEALING THE WOUND
OF OUR DIVISION

Divisiveness in mainstream Protestantism is a wound that must be healed if we are to recover from our malnourished condition. In his study of American church development since World War II, Robert Wuthnow says: "For anyone with even a casual knowledge of American religious history the present divide between religious conservatives and religious liberals may sound much like the controversy between fundamentalism and modernism that brewed into a major cultural conflict around the beginning of the present century. Indeed, one interpretation of the current divide that appears to be fairly widely subscribed to holds that the present controversy grows directly out of the earlier conflict."[1] This conflict must be faced if we are healed of our malnourished condition.

Let us now briefly recapitulate. Mainstream Protestantism is held at bay because church leaders are intellectually and emotionally paralyzed by the threat of three cultural features that our own traditions have spawned: *fundamentalism, scientism, and greedy materialism.* Our belief system is malnourished because we no longer obtain nourishment from the Bible. We find less and less help in traditional theologies rooted in the Bible. We lost the Bible as our bonding agent because we did not develop enough teachers in our churches with competence to teach it as it must be taught. Those who have been able to keep up with biblical studies might make the mistake of assuming that everyone has been able to do the same.

It will be a disaster if a few leaders assume, for any reason, that what is "old stuff" to them is also "old stuff" to the entire membership.

Millions of American mainstream Protestants would welcome an alternative to biblical literalism. The psychologization of religion resulted in a shortage of trained pastors who know the Bible well enough to teach it as it must be taught now. Untrained lay people cannot teach the Bible. Development of effective teaching of the Bible cannot succeed until all five of our leadership castes see the urgent need for competent teachers, clergy, and laity. When we discover in hermeneutic conversations how far behind we have fallen, we will be cured of our paralysis by the singular discovery that a recovery of Jesus' message means more in our time than it did in his own time. Neither liberals nor fundamentalists can now claim that we have properly understood or proclaimed Jesus.

We must make a wholesale advance in our communication methods. We must face together the realities brought to us in the new knowledge about the Bible and Jesus. New viewpoints are difficult to learn because one may have to unlearn some cherished views. The new biblical knowledge is ten times harder to communicate because it usually contradicts what people have been taught. Furthermore, our church members have become literalists in reading newspapers and journals.

Not many of our people are trained to appreciate literature that does not deal with purported facts and hard data. Few among us read poetry or appreciate the way that language can nurture the spirit with more than logical analysis or statistics. Not many people can benefit from the superior delights of going beyond the words on a printed page. Mainstream Protestantism has before it the mighty task of helping people to understand the Bible as a literature of the human spirit in its quest for life's meanings. We also have before us the necessity of managing a theological revolution—long overdue.

Healing the wound of our division begins when leaders liberate their minds to imagine what great values are ahead if we walk together. We can find our bonding agent in a fresh, mutual appreciation for the Bible. We can explore new meanings for our lives in adventurous theology loosed from antique formulations. We should laugh off our past history and say together that both liberals and fundamentalists are now obsolete. New knowledge about the Bible (by no means "old stuff" to more than a few) requires that we learn to see our Bible together through new eyes and open hearts.

The bleeding wound caused by our conflict over the Bible makes assimilation of more nourishing beliefs impossible. Mainstream Protestants have intuitively valued difference of theological viewpoint. I am not arguing for theological agreement. We will not find our healing in agreements. We will find our healing through understanding one another.

If we can openly explore together what the new knowledge of the Bible means now, then we can become more open to the Spirit of God. We must learn how to become biblical characters in our own time. We must appreciate the Bible as our memory of the human spirit in its quest to serve God by using freedom intelligently for moral growth in caring for the world. This is what our Bible calls us to do.

UNDERSTANDING, NOT COMPROMISE

Our usual way of handling conflicting opinions is to have one side win or both sides enter into a compromise. This approach must be buried forever. The pronouncement of truth by a majority vote is not for us in mainstream Protestantism. It is for us to demonstrate the power of mutuality by understanding one another. This is the harder way. But we must be willing to follow a harder way and to understand one another in depth. In hermeneutic conversations about the Bible, theology, and social ethics, liberals and fundamentalists will find richer perceptions of essential Christian living. We must practice this spiritual art on a church-wide basis. We must recover the Bible as our healing and bonding agent. We must learn to enjoy theology as the highest employment of logic wedded to poetry and prayer.

In order to be our binding agent, the Bible must accomplish

specific functions. George Lindbeck of Yale Divinity School says that the Bible achieves its bonding power by providing

> texts projecting imaginatively and practically habitable worlds. . . . A habitable text must in some fashion be construable as a guide to thought and action in the encounter with changing circumstances. It must supply followable directions for coherent patterns of life in new situations. If it does this, it can be considered rational to dwell within it; no other foundations are necessary, or, in the contemporary climate of opinion, possible.[2]

On the contrary, the Bible cannot offer us "habitable worlds" or "guides to thought and action." The Bible is pre-scientific in origin. How can it possibly offer us "practically habitable worlds"? Maybe it could do that for Martin Luther or John Wesley, but they did not live in our world of nuclear weapons and laser mysteries.

Why are we not already at work to heal our wound? Why have we not moved rapidly forward to make possible a continuing use of the Bible as a source for "followable directions for coherent patterns of life in new situations"? We officially admit that strict literalism is not for us. What are we putting into its place? The modernist approach to the Bible was deficient. We have remnants of biblical literalism in our body to weaken us more every day. Why are we paralyzed so that we do not attend to our own healing?

This question brings us to a delicate point. The psychologization of religion has influenced the education of significant numbers of church leaders in key leadership positions. Under the pressures of learning what they were required to know about psychology and related subjects, many leaders were not able to keep up with their biblical and theological studies. Local congregations wanted psychologized religion, and pastors and others were trained to meet their expectations. Biblical studies and theology lost out in the competition with psychologized religion.

What is the proof that this is so? One solid indicator is the sale of books and journals on biblical or theological subjects, which hover between 3,000 to 4,000 copies. Another example is *Quarterly Review: A Journal of Scholarly Reflection for the Ministry.* Published by The United Methodist Church for professional leaders, this journal is heavily subsidized. This excellent quarterly had 2,488 paid subscriptions at the end of 1989. There are about 38,000 United Methodist pastors. Only .6 percent of these pastors (less than 250) are subscribers. Other mainstream denominations have an equally sad story.

After encouragement from ecumenical agencies, The United Methodist Church launched the *International Christian Digest* in October 1986. It had an excellent editorial staff, a fine layout, and bold plans to make substantial articles from all around the world handy for the church leader. It lasted three years and was quietly terminated in October 1989. What happened? Not enough subscribers after extensive promotion.

What about books? At the end of 1989, the *Christian Century* reported a survey of its subscribers. One item dealt with the book-buying patterns of its audience, which is mainly clergy from the higher-income range—with an average household income of $49,800. Nearly half of its subscribers live in cities of one hundred thousand or more. On average, these highly privileged leaders buy twenty-three books a year. This contrasts sharply with one book publisher whose survey of pastors as a wholesale lot revealed a purchase of fewer than three books per year. Leaders may use borrowed books, of course, but how many books would be available for borrowing if nobody were buying? We have reason to fear that our church leaders in all five castes have fallen behind in biblical and theological studies.

Every church leader cannot be a specialized scholar. The most that we can expect from systematic exchanges between our leaders and our theological faculties is the development of a spiritual mood—a redeemed intention—resulting in a better flow of nourishing beliefs into our organizational life. We cannot be healed until we find a higher mutuality in our leadership castes which is born of new learning.

This higher mutuality demands a post-modern understanding of the Bible. Such terms as *post-industrial, post-civilizational,* and even *post-modern* need definition. A good definition of a post-modernistic view is given to us by Edgar V. McKnight in his *Post-Modern Use of the Bible*.[3] In his final chapter he delineates the three roles that a reader of the Bible must learn to take. The first role is to actualize the verbal content of the text. The second role is to refer the text or theme to an occasion of contemporary significance. The third role is to actualize the text while reading. This sounds very complex in this condensed description. However, when we "act out" the three roles, the process seems as natural as breathing. In planned hermeneutic conversations, such uses of the Bible as McKnight proposes could be demonstrated far enough to make them a clear basis for mutuality between liberal and fundamentalist views of the Bible.

I am under no illusions that McKnight's book will become popular reading, even in top leadership castes. It is a technical book for trained scholars, but it can be made communicable to the average reader if we decide to take seriously the task of using methods already known outside the church—methods ignored by our churches on a grand scale. The mainstream Protestant churches are close to the bottom ranks of contemporary organizations when it comes to communicating ideas.

Lindbeck's "habitable world" and his "followable directions for coherent patterns of life in new situations" have much in common with McKnight's "actualization." Both writers demand great concentration from the reader. We must find new ways to make ideas more easily available to our leaders and our members. Too much of our new knowledge is not in a communicable form. Our scholars do not write for us; they write for one another. William F. Fore has been pleading this issue for years. Formerly on the staff of the National Council of Churches and more recently on the faculty of Yale Divinity School, Fore has pleaded for the church to use effective methods to convey knowledge to the membership.[4] If industry and the military can learn to train people in weeks instead of years, then we mainstream Protestants can do even better because we have millions of dedicated, eager leaders ready to move forward.

We have seen that organizations cannot remain healthy unless energies received are digested and then expressed in actions that the members believe in supporting. Our spiritual and moral energies must find expression in ways that connect us to great social purposes. We are all human beings, which means we have needs for the realization of social hopes. It will be very dangerous if church leaders confine emphasis to subjective experience. Biblical faith links a subjective meditation to a life expressed in social hopes. The healing of our wounds requires social actions to be rooted in our faith that God is with us, requiring us to achieve goals we could never achieve without God's help. To be Christians we must together work for a world that is better than it is. Christians are theological idealists who happily choose risky adventure for Christ's sake.

Where do we find new goals to fit our needs? We might turn to Africa, Asia, or Latin America. We could focus on America, that land of such great wealth and rampant greediness. Our gross materialism troubles all of us. There is a nationwide distress at the sight of Americans hopelessly lost in our American adventure of high consumer goods productivity. We mainstream Protestants should not be held at bay by this. We must not be paralyzed in the face of such evil. Our joy will be found in a united challenge of the materialism we have done so much to spawn. We should be ready to discipline our own offspring and to think of our labors as our obedience to God.

We have been thrown off the true course of our discipleship. We are not hypocrites. We are not unfaithful. But we are brought up sharply by our declining vitality and membership losses. Is this altogether bad? Is the wound we suffer a fatal wound? Is our malnourished condition today the end of us? In spite of my own considerable dismay at our plight, I am convinced that the best thing that could ever have happened to us in the middle of the twentieth century has happened.

We had become smugly proud of our organizations' successes. Our failures to see what we had done to spawn fundamentalism, greedy materialism, and narrow scientism expose our shallowness. We mainstream Protestants are now forced to reconsider how we read the Bible, understand Jesus, think of God, and find true obedience as human beings on a fragile planet. We have been forced to our knees, and painful as it may be, it is the best thing that could happen to us. We needed to be purged of our obsolete and deficient belief system.

While we have been floundering in recent years, something of great promise has been developing. Since 1930, new information about Jesus has been flooding in upon us. This new information is not widely spread. Failure to be involved together in exploring new scholarship about Jesus will aggravate our division, thereby worsening our wound. Recent studies require reconsideration of many widely held conceptions.

We must take immediate steps to engage all of our leadership castes in hermeneutic conversations about Jesus. When we have helped one another appreciate the new studies about Jesus, we must discover ways of bringing our entire membership along with us. This may be the most demanding task we have ever undertaken.

The next chapter is a one-sided hermeneutic conversation about recovering Jesus for our living today. It is what I would take into a hermeneutic conversation as of this moment. The reader will supply another view. If we could share in deep hermeneutic conversation, then my experience of Jesus as the "Parable of God" would be enhanced.

CHAPTER
VI

THE RECOVERY OF JESUS

We cannot involve our church members in reading the Bible as literature without encountering questions about Jesus. What about his birth, miracles, resurrection, and second coming? Who was he? What did he say? How can we know that he said it? Careful readers of the New Testament know how often one gospel writer quotes Jesus as saying something that contradicts what another gospel writer quotes him as saying. We cannot simply open the Bible and find the authentic Jesus. Whether or not we can find the authentic Jesus is a legitimate question, and it should be openly recognized that our best scholars are locked in debate on this question.

NEW SCHOLARSHIP

When the twentieth century was born, an entirely new approach to the study of who Jesus was already had gotten under way. Albert Schweitzer is known by most people as a medical missionary, but New Testament scholars praise him for his book *The Quest for the Historical Jesus* (trans. 1910). Schweitzer argued that our knowledge of Jesus is limited, but we can at least know that his message was mainly about the way things end. Jesus is seen by Schweitzer as an eschatological preacher.

The new biblical scholarship really got under way with C. H. Dodd's *The Parables of the Kingdom* (1935). This book opened up much that Schweitzer had missed. Then Joachim

Jeremias built on Dodd's work to produce *The Parables of Jesus* (1954). This work was revised in 1962, and again in 1973, to keep it abreast of developments. New Testament scholarship today has gone far beyond Schweitzer, Dodd, Jeremias, and others whose work launched a great movement forward in New Testament studies.

Theological schools have scholars who are at work in various areas of research such as manuscript analysis, linguistics, the new hermeneutical perceptions, and historical verification through anthropology, archaeology, and other disciplines. There has probably never been a period in the history of Christianity when so much effort has been concentrated on recovering something authentic about who Jesus really was and what Jesus really proclaimed.

Not that anyone hopes we will ever have a biography of Jesus. In any case, biographies are notably tricky sources for truth about people, and it is no great loss that we have no biography of Jesus. We have differing biographies about each of our founding fathers, but we know them best through what they wrote or said. It seems clear that what we may know about Jesus will be through recovering something of what he said, and here is where we must depend on reports by others. This means we are forced into cautious study of what others say that Jesus said.

Fiction writers and film makers will inevitably find ways to tickle public interest about a fictional figure they will call Jesus. He holds a distinctive role in human history, and there is always a waiting audience. But the mainstream Protestants cannot indulge in creating a fictional Jesus who then serves as a contrived energy source for their organized worship and service of God. Christians need to know with real confidence that their beliefs associated with Jesus are valid.

The real question about Jesus is whether he knew anything or experienced anything that can help us make sense out of this precarious and consequential existence in which we must make choices. Did Jesus ever say anything that points us to that "habitable world" where we feel we are at home through time and into eternity? Is there anything about Jesus that brings us to understand or experience God in a personal way while we also understand our universe in scientific terms Jesus never heard of? Is there anything about Jesus that can bring us into a living relationship with the Ultimate Reality so that we can make sense out of the daily confusions we inevitably must deal with? These are all shapes of the same question: Can Jesus help us find meaning for our lives? Can we know Jesus, and through this knowing be helped to enter into a vital relationship with God? Can Jesus help us achieve true epiphany?

In order to answer questions of this dimension, we must first refresh our minds with what we know today about Jesus. We must begin with the few facts about Jesus that are indisputable. We first admit that:

> Jesus was a Galilean peasant who wrote nothing. His native tongue was Aramaic, whereas the records of what he said, created later by others, exist only in Greek, with a few texts in further translation preserved in Latin, or Coptic, or other ancient language. The tradition has preserved only a few Aramaic words attributed to Jesus. Accordingly, if Jesus spoke only in Aramaic, his original words have been lost forever. The words of Jesus recorded in the gospels are thus at best a translation from Aramaic into Greek or some other ancient tongue.[1]

In addition to the problem of having nothing written by Jesus' own hand, we have great complications associated with interpreting manuscripts of the Gospels we now have. Although we now habitually date Mark at about 70 c.e., with Matthew and Luke–Acts at about 85 c.e. and John at about 95 c.e., we do not have any complete manuscripts of these Gospels that are earlier than 200 c.e. Thus, our oldest records about Jesus are from manuscripts written two centuries after he was crucified.

There are other problems that add to the difficulty. The early Christians were probably very much like the other people of their own day in most respects. They shared the commonly held beliefs and opinions about sickness and health, birth and death, gods and demons. Strongly held notions framed in legends and myths were elements that shaped their views of the world. It was inevitable that each Christian writer brought into the record not only the oral traditions about Jesus but also his own personal understanding of what those traditions meant. It is inevitable that any human being will speak of the world in terms of the prevailing wisdom (science, legends, or myths) of his or her own time.

The New Testament is a reflection of an early community of believers. It is the formulation of what their convictions required. They reinforced their formulations of belief in liturgy and celebrations. All of this together gave them guidance in daily behavior. Brevard Childs has given us a rich description of how these written records became the official documentation of a community of believers who needed a screened collection of what they considered to be most worthy and of highest authority.[2] They valued what helped them make sense out of their world, what made their world habitable.

Language and Meaning

Now let us take notice of two things that have accompanied the rise of increased desire to account for the authentic voice of Jesus. One development asks what form the language takes; the other development asks how that form conveys meaning.

Most of us avoid technical discussions about language. We use language every day and do very well with it, so why bother with technical details? If we let ourselves become too self-conscious about the form that our speech is taking, then we often become confused and stumble. Children often invent marvelous word pictures by using language as they see fit. This reveals to us how speech may have distinctive characteristics in each of us. Some of us have a definitive personal style which can be distinguished rather easily from the styles of speech or writing typical of others. Each gospel writer has a style that is quite distinct, as any careful reader of the Gospels has already noticed.

There is another side to this. When we examine how language is structured and how it conveys meaning from one person to another, we must stand in awe of the great wonder that human beings can communicate with one another. In our own time, the discoveries of ancient manuscripts come together with notable advances in our understanding of how language (written and spoken) functions in our lives.

Biblical studies have been plunged into a study of language structure by everything that has happened after Jülicher's astute reminder in 1895 that a parable isn't the same as an allegory. First in Europe and then increasingly in the United States, the work of New Testament scholars has been linked to the labors of specialists in language analysis. Among these scholars who have a greater than average interest in New Testament literature is Amos N. Wilder, whose essays broke new ground in understanding parables.[3] When Norman Perrin of the University of Chicago published *Jesus and the Language of the Kingdom* in 1976,[4] he advanced Wilder's argument that, in the parables, we have Jesus speaking in metaphors that are stretched into stories in some cases. Furthermore, the authentic voice of the real Jesus is in his use of *Kingdom of God* as a symbol. It is used by Jesus to evoke the listener's attention to the way that God is acting in the world now and in the future.

In the same year that *Jesus and the Language of the Kingdom* was published, Perrin also issued *Recovering the Teachings of Jesus.*[5] It is quite obvious that he had been working on these two books so that they might come out at the same time. Their publication at that time was fortunate. There was great need for some scholar of competence to pull things together. The advances had been so fast and on so many fronts that most students of the New Testament needed a good overview, and Perrin's work helped.

Effects of New Scholarship

This New Testament scholarship has stirred up some heated controversy. For increasing numbers of people it has made biblical literalism a larger issue than it has been before now. The evidence is increasing that many teachings attributed to Jesus were put into his lips by devout followers who also glorified and amplified accounts about what Jesus had done. These anecdotes stuck to Jesus like burrs. In the same way that hero stories cling to Abraham Lincoln and George Washington, heroic tales stuck to Jesus, and the early Christians formed their *aretalogy*—their collection of heroic tales. Without the tales, the Gospels as we have them would not have become treasures of the religious community.

At the same time, the authentic Jesus has been buried in the confusion. Contemporary biblical studies have brought us to the very difficult stage where the Jesus of our literal interpretations simply is not viable any more. We are brought face to face with the charge that the New Testament is a fraud. It is a fraud, some might charge, because it purports to be historical truth when, in fact, it is not. There are some very hard questions being asked about Jesus today, and mainstream Protestantism must define good answers.

We mainstream leaders know that the questions are there. We also know the difficulties of facing the rank and file membership with answers because those answers seem too technical (unorthodox) to explain. Many leaders are good enough students of the Bible and theology to know that the answers are there. They have found the answers good for their own minds and hearts. The big trouble is the unorthodox and complex nature of the answers as they are presently formulated. We have not yet learned how to simplify explanations and develop clear images that our church members can quickly grasp. Many leaders who know the results of scholarship may have concluded that the material is too complicated for anyone but the scholars.

The big mainstream Protestant task in communication is to develop skills that convey to the membership these new discoveries about the authentic voice of Jesus and to make clear, even to small children, how the biblical narratives convey the authentic voice of Jesus through twenty centuries of turbulence. To accomplish this goal we must first change our ways of thinking about the Bible. Many mainstream leaders dread the possibility that advanced studies about Jesus will upset our membership and cause more people to leave our churches. Our old fundamentalistic views of Jesus hold mainstream Protestants at bay, and leaders are paralyzed by new truth that upsets old dogmas.

Many of us have been strengthened by the new information

about Jesus. We know this information is fragmentary, incomplete, and subject to change as new learning forces new recognitions of angles overlooked. But we have been helped by it. If we are helped by it, then should we not assume that it will help others as much as it helps us? To deal with this question more specifically, let us look at a sketch of what Jesus is like when we strip things down to the bare minimum of what we think, today, that we can know for sure about Jesus.

JESUS: PARABLE OF GOD

Jesus is known to us through the parables. They proclaim the way God is reigning in the world now and in the future. The parables were used by Jesus to evoke in the minds and hearts of his hearers a consciousness of the reigning power that is acting now and in the future on all people and upon all events. Jesus used parables to talk about how God reigns in the world. He tantalizes us and arouses our latent insights. The parables "get into us" because they evoke what is already stirring within our hearts and minds. They "speak to our condition." The Kingdom of God in the parables is the symbol of the way God is acting in the procession of events and occasions.

At the same time, the parables do not force answers on us. When Jesus speaks in parables, we are stirred to new awareness; but we are not handed a theology. The most popular phrase among scholars describing what parables do is simply "they tease our minds."

The parable of the leaven (Matthew 13:33b) is known around the world. How comic it is. Visualize a little leaven activating something like fifty pounds of flour in a Palestinian kitchen! That would make enough bread to feed a hundred people. This parable teases our minds to think of the way God reigns in the world. It does not tell us something. Instead, it evokes something within us. The little parable awakens us to the unexamined but tantalizing possibilities in God who is reigning now. All of the parables do the same thing. Parables *do* something.

But have we really recovered Jesus? What about the Virgin

Birth, the Divine Savior, the Word of God who became flesh and dwelt among us? Where is the miracle worker, the man who was crucified and then raised from the tomb to walk on the shore in a resurrected body? There is a list of questions that must be answered, and they have clear answers. All of these questions and more must have better answers than we have been handing out for centuries. This is a new day for Jesus in the modern world.

Fortunately, the best contemporary scholarship offers better ways to think about Jesus. We are being given new answers that take us far beyond biblical literalism. These better answers undergird our appreciation for Jesus as a unique person in the evolution of history. These answers deliver us from saying that Jesus was born into this world by supernatural actions. We see him in new answers as the fruit of God's presence in the processes of the world. I see great gain in understanding Jesus as a man who was born as we are born. He loved and lived as a true human being. In his humanity he is unique in his own way, just as each of us is unique in our own way.

He spoke in parables as none other has ever spoken. They evoke in us a continuing variety of images of how God is working in our world. His earthly presence lives in our midst as a walking parable of God. There is religious genius in the Fourth Gospel's depiction of Jesus as the Word that became flesh and dwelt among us. "Jesus the parable of God" is an amplified conception of "Jesus the Word" proclaiming God in the language each of us can understand: a loving human being who gives his life for others.

I dare to offer a myth.

In the beginning, when God had allowed the earth to be among the stars and planets, God touched the earth and allowed human life to form. This human life was formed out of the stuff of the universe to become an intelligent being. Human life was given freedom to use the gift of intelligence for either good or evil. Human capacity to do evil things was boundless. Intelligence was used destructively. So God waited, and in due time God chose to speak to the human creatures who had become very numerous. But God did not

115

speak in Greek, French, German, or English. God spoke in the language of a human form, and his name was called Jesus. He lived the life of self-giving love and suffered a violent death without striking back. And the whole world is hushed to this day by the presence of Jesus, who is the parable of God in life.

Jesus is the Word that God continuously speaks. He troubles us more than we admit, because he upsets our plans and invites us to give our lives to others. His promise is epiphany: the union with God that we crave with our soul and body crying out.

The parables always seem to speak of two things at the same time: judgment and grace. These words are difficult to define. Judgment can mean the inevitable tangle of consequences that follow from what we say or do. A sober driver may run over a pedestrian and face the same consequences as if he had been drunk. A group of physicists contrive an atomic bomb. It is dropped on a city, killing thousands they never intended to murder. Life is provocative with its subtle quandaries. In a similar way, the parables of Jesus are always laden with the provocative atmosphere of consequence not defined in detail, but God's judgment is always present or implied as present.

Although an atmosphere of judgment pervades the parables, there is another quality about them. The parables of Jesus evoke our understanding of grace, generosity, and forgiveness. But these wonderful gifts are never free. They must be bought by penitence. The vineyard workers (Matthew 20:1-15) are generously rewarded for unequal hours of labor in the hot sun. Underneath is the tone of judgment on the grumblers who resent the graciousness of the man who owns the vineyard. This parable is a precarious piece because it lends itself to vivid allegorization. But if we hold back from twisting it into an allegory, it takes us far beyond payrolls and sour early birds greedy for an extra coin. The parable speaks to us about the way that God gives graciously whether or not we merit the graciousness we receive, while at the same time it points to grumbling greediness.

Mainstream Protestant leaders should enlist the entire church membership in the new quest for the authentic Jesus.

This could be one of the boldest moves ever made by the Christian church. Our belief system will be nourished by a genuine church-wide hermeneutic conversation involving scholars and all leadership castes in a shared quest for the authentic voice of Jesus.

We must gain the necessary courage to examine our entire educational curriculum. Hermeneutic conversations will help us gather the courage to weed out of our study materials everything that goes beyond what we really have a right to say that we know about Jesus. This is going to be much harder than it sounds. It will require fine distinctions on the part of editors and writers. Almost all of our current study materials present a false Jesus to our mainstream church members.

The educational program in our church should not tell children or adults things about Jesus that are legendary and tell those things as if they were facts. All Bible scholars know of the great contradictions between the Nativity Story in Luke and the one found in Matthew. What the scholars know, little children should be taught. These birth narratives are only a handy example—and the simplest of them all. But there should be a dedicated effort to bring people into an appreciation of the great legends and myths of the Bible, while at the same time showing even the youngest child that these legends and myths do not pretend to be factual accounts. They have had their distinctive functions in the past. They can have distinctive value now if we take the trouble to help children and adults understand the way legends and myths contribute to spiritual living.

The theological schools of mainstream Protestantism abandoned long ago the supernaturalism commonly associated with the birth, life, and death of Jesus. We leaders of the mainstream churches dread the very thought of providing alternates to the prevailing superstitions about Jesus, even though these false teachings impede real understanding of who Jesus was and is today. The arduous work of leading the mainstream Protestants in a correction of our faded traditions about Jesus requires more than we feel able to give. Our own internal remnants of fundamentalistic doctrines about Jesus paralyze us. We are holding back from providing the nourishment that our churches must have if Jesus is to be sustained as a saving presence in our community of faith.

Changes in curriculum materials always mean conflict with those who have held control over contents of educational materials. In all mainstream denominations the educational material about Jesus is couched in terms of ideas and language that will not upset anyone. The reason is practical. The local church leaders in charge of buying these materials are people who have stayed with the mainstream church school programs because they have no trouble believing that the programs are acceptable. Whenever any of the material departs from their own settled views, church leaders quit buying from the denominational source and turn to the fundamentalist press. Some of these are straight commercial enterprises that go out of their way to satisfy a market no matter what kind of material they must publish. The recovery of Jesus in our educational materials will not come without conflict over who controls the content of these materials. Leaders are seldom capable of making radical changes in their written materials unless there is an audience obviously waiting for the changes to come. We will never have suitable educational materials on all levels in our churches until there has been a development of desire for better materials. The development of a desire for better materials will not be born until hermeneutic conversations about the new knowledge of Jesus are taking place on every level in our mainstream Protestant churches.

The difficulty of our task is equalled only by the urgency of it. The Bible cannot be our bonding agent in mainstream Protestantism until our people learn how to benefit from its mixtures of fact, fiction, legend, myth, poetry, parable and allegory. Jesus cannot be real for us as Lord and Savior unless we recover him from burial beneath "dusty legends and myths." We mainstream Protestants cannot afford to stand idly and wait for secular publications to do our educating for us.

In its August 15, 1988 issue, *Time* magazine ran six pages of discussion on who Jesus was. This was at the time when Scorsese's film *The Last Temptation of Christ* had aroused a public furor because of its portrayal of Jesus as a man who was tempted by a woman and whose revolution failed. The article included a sketchy summary of some of the recent developments in New Testament scholarship. These were mentioned with subtle insertions of editorial comment by the magazine's writers. The *Time* article illustrates the temper of the times, and so does Scorsese's film. These discussions prove that there is real interest in a better understanding of Jesus in terms that help us find meaning for our daily living. We mainstream Protestant churches have an opportunity that we have never had before. We can now put Jesus right into the heart of the evolutionary process of human development and speak of him as the truly human, the Word become flesh, the parable of God.

Most people apparently think of the Gospels as biographies of Jesus. When they discover how much the Gospels vary in important details about who Jesus was, they may discover their own ways to harmonize those differences. When Scorsese's film went beyond anything in either Gospel to present a purely fictional Jesus, many were outraged. There is a genuine sensitivity in the minds of most Americans when they think of Jesus. Hermeneutic conversations about Jesus hold great promise for linking the resident sensitivity that we feel toward Jesus with our enduring desire to know what the New Testament reports about what Jesus means for us now.

We mainstream Protestants have a major task ahead of us if we bring Jesus into our organizational life as an energy source. Our malnourished belief systems cannot be fed on the thin gruel of a stained-glass Jesus. Nor can our belief systems find nourishment if Jesus is diminished until he is a disillusioned revolutionary who lost his cause and his followers and was rescued by only a fabricated tale about his resuscitation from death. What we have ahead of us is a radical penetration into our own failures to appreciate fully what happened in the evolution of the human race when Jesus of Nazareth broke into history and became more real after his crucifixion than he had ever been before he was tortured and slain.

The reality of this drama of Jesus, the parable of God, is our Christian heritage. It helps us transform belief into faith. The time seems ripe for an intense concentration of hermeneutic conversations with biblical scholars, linguistic specialists, historians, mainstream Protestant church leaders, and our whole rank and file membership to help put Jesus into the heart of evolutionary history where he belongs as our inspiration and guide.

No sooner will we be embarked on this promising pilgrimage in mainstream Protestantism than we will discover that Jesus is requiring us now to think again about the immediate immanence of God and the significance of a whole ecological ethic.

CHAPTER
VII

THE IMMEDIATE IMMANENCE OF GOD AND A WHOLE ECOLOGICAL ETHIC

New knowledge about the world forces changes in theology. The most noticeable pressure for thinking about God is coming from the women who have grown weary of the focus on God as male. Although there are many very competent female theologians who could be cited in this connection, here we refer only to Sally McFague of Vanderbilt Divinity School. Among her books is *Models of God: Theology for an Ecological, Nuclear Age.*[1] She proposes that we displace the masculine Trinity (Father, Son, Holy Spirit) with a feminine Trinity (Mother, Friend, Lover). This specific suggestion is rounded out with arguments to show that such a model for thinking of God is much more likely to help us sustain a theology for an "ecological, nuclear age."

James Moulder, who says that he is unable to believe in God because he has found no convincing arguments, also says that feminist theology only makes him more agnostic. He thinks that Sally McFague's solution is no solution at all because it substitutes one mystification for another.[2]

After benefiting from discussions of this kind and quality, it is now time for us to take another look at the Bible and our theology in the light of our best scholarship. This scholarship does not, of course, present us with a solid block of consensus. For the very reason that both theology and biblical studies are in a state of change, I am pleading for a fusion of the church leadership system with our theological faculties in systematic hermeneutic conversations.

121

Let us imagine for a moment that Sally McFague and James Moulder are in the same hermeneutic conversation group, along with about twenty other church leaders. Given the agreement that neither will try to win an argument, what chance is there that they would be able to find any common ground for discourse? At first it might seem that none can possibly be found. But let us take another small imaginative step to find each person in the conversation explaining how he or she understands the Bible's portrayal of God.

IMMEDIATE IMMANENCE

It seems clear that from beginning to end in the Bible there is a sustained emphasis on God as an acting presence in the way the world works and the ways people must act if they hope to establish a decent world fit for God's children to walk in. Regardless of whatever else the Bible may say about God, hermeneutic conversations will inevitably come to the point where the immediate immanence of God in events is given emphasis.

Nowhere else in the Bible is this immediate immanence of God in the procession of events more clearly evoked than in the parables of Jesus. As noted in the previous chapter, the parables evoke our awareness of how God is acting. Jesus speaks to us through the parables as an authentic voice which awakens us to what we already seem to know in some fragmentary way. We know that the leaven works in the lump of dough, but the parable evokes in us the knowledge that God is leaven in the lumps of experience which either threaten us or give us hope.

The immediate immanence of God in the biblical literature cannot be limited to either gender. I think we owe feminist theologians a great debt because they have challenged the narrowness of a masculine view of God. I am fully aware of the stubborn reality of the Bible's predominantly masculine imagery for God. Because I am not a biblical literalist, I discount those patriarchal terms. But why, then, should we pay attention to the biblical emphasis on the immediate immanence of God? Why not just abandon the Bible?

The Bible is a literary treasure which serves as a carrier of our ancestral memory of a quest for God. A dominant feature of this ancestral memory is the immediate immanence of God in history. It is the task of mainstream Protestantism to bring the Bible back into use and to clarify how the Bible is our cultural memory of the immediate immanence of God continuously sustaining the achievement of a moral use of human intelligence and freedom. Liberating the Bible from the constraints of literalism and endowing it with the fullness of profound literature of the heart and soul, of mind and strength, and of striving human spirits can bring nourishment into our malnourished mainstream church life.

MODELS OF GOD

In any serious hermeneutic conversation involving the leaders of our five caste systems and our theological faculties, it is inevitable that there must be a discussion of what Sally McFague and Ian Barbour[3] call "models of God." It also seems inevitable that deeply serious hermeneutic conversations will find movement away from limiting God to either masculine or feminine terms. The movement beyond gender terminology means more than may first meet the eye. It seems that the model or conception of God has moved beyond personality as such. It means that the theology of personalism is transcended.

But how can we think of God in terms higher than *Person*? This question has been asked all through the twentieth century, and it has not been given a satisfying answer because almost no one has been asking what kind of word *G-O-D* is. Does the word *G-O-D* have to refer to a person-like God? To be sure, the Bible does this throughout. For example, consider the Song of the Vineyard from Isaiah 5:1-4. Surely, this is one of the more beautiful passages in the Bible, and it is masculine and handsomely personalized:

I shall sing for my beloved my love song about his vineyard:
My beloved had a vineyard high up on a fertile slope.
He trenched it, cleared it of stone, and planted it with choice
red vines; in the middle he built a watch-tower and also
hewed out a wine vat.
He expected it to yield choice grapes, but all it yielded was a
crop of wild grapes. (NREB)

Masculine though it may be, do we not agree that the central emphasis is not on the gender of the singer but on the tragedy of the broken hopes the singer suffers?

In spite of the largely masculine representation of God in the Bible, it is not an essential paradigm to speak of God as either masculine, feminine, or person-like. The biblical narrative unfolds its drama of human life with a consistent yearning for human obedience to God whose Being is not limited to the attributes of personality. God is more than person. The Bible transcends its personalism by genuine portrayal of the Creator of persons. This is the eternal "more than person" we must learn to capture in language. We must learn, then, to focus on the biblical theme that is central: human beings striving to achieve a moral use of their freedom and intelligence.

An excellent illustration of this note which is so consistent in the Bible is the narrative of Israel's escape from bondage in Egypt. From Egypt to Sinai we see Israel burdened by a freedom they did not know how to use! Even with the legendary Moses and his legendary tablets of stone engraved with divine laws, the people continue to misuse their freedom. Their national failures and even their daily human ills are explained in terms of their failure to use freedom responsibly in a world of moral consequences.

When we talk about the immediate immanence of God in the way things work together in the world, we are forced to find new formulations that will enable us to speak of God acting in the procession of evolutionary events. We can do this only if we are able to relax long enough to agree that there is nothing sacred about the term *G-O-D* in the sense that we cannot doubt what we have thought or change our minds about what we once believed. Indeed, when we develop enough freedom in our hermeneutic conversation to agree that the term *G-O-D* is a generic concept and is used by people whenever they speak of ultimate power or powers upon which life depends, we have established our basis for hermeneutic conversation about God.

If I am convinced that there are powers in tea leaves or stars that determine my health or good fortune in marriage, then I am thinking about God in those terms. If I believe strongly that the world is a cosmic accident—produced in a wild explosion—and will come to a cataclysmic end in a dark hole, then I may not admit that I am thinking about God, but I am thinking about ultimate things. In human discourse, this puts me into the ranks of those who think about God—even if I am agnostic about God being male, female, all-powerful, aloof from the world, or existent at all.

We mainstream Protestants have a strong enough history of freedom of inquiry to engage in some very heady hermeneutic conversations about God as the immediately immanent power that cannot be trifled with. Against the background of the biblical narrative culminating in the parables of Jesus, we are called to examine in new ways how our personal and social behavior is caught between God's immediate immanence on one side and our reckless uses of science-based technology on the other.

AN ADEQUATE THEOLOGY FOR A NEW ETHIC

The basis for a Christian theology to sustain the emerging ecological ethic is laid in the Bible and is given force by the emphasis Jesus gives to God's rule in the Kingdom which is forever God's: now and in the future. It is our job now to give the theological articulation to what we know about the way this world works and how our future is tied into the ways that we use our freedom and intelligence. To put it more bluntly, it is time for mainstream Protestants to assume responsibility and to take the lead in saying that there are some things human beings cannot do without encountering God's everlasting "thou shalt not." The earth is not ours, human life is not ours, and God cannot be trifled with in a universe of consequential events. To do this effectively in our preaching and teaching ministries, we must make radical changes in the ways that we talk about God and the Bible. These radical changes cannot be achieved by books or articles in journals. They must be hammered out in the laborious work of hermeneutic conversations involving all five levels of our leadership caste system and all of our theological faculties.

The psychologization of the Christian religion during the past fifty years has sentimentalized and trivialized mainstream Protestant faith. The cheap mouthing of how God loves us no matter who we are or what we do is repudiated by biblical narrative and the symbol of the cross. It may be true that God loves all of creation and everyone in it, but when this is taken to mean approval for any kind of behavior and all modes of living, it mocks Christian faith.

Luis Maria Saumells exhibited his screen print of *The Creator* in Frankfurt, New York, Chicago, and Madrid in the early 1960s. He was a young man in Barcelona during the terrible Spanish Civil War. His portrait of God is a fiercely indignant countenance with creative fires lighting deep eyes fixed on all who dare to look. In God's left hand the world is held, embraced with fingers hardly seen. The right hand is held palm outward, warning us to either stop or move with caution. I cannot escape from its power of projecting the immediate immanence of God, demanding of all human creatures a more responsible use of their intelligence and freedom.

But there is also promise in this powerful work of art, as there is promise in all theology that speaks soberly of God's immediate immanence in the world, and as there is promise in the parables of Jesus and the biblical literature. It is the promise of rewarding outcomes. Fruit rewards faithfulness in the vineyard.

We mainstream Protestants have been flogging ourselves upward and onward to achieve a high social ethic. We have "lamented" and "regretted" our "manifold sins and wicked ness" with regularity. What we must evolve out of our hermeneutic conversation about God is an understanding of the sacredness of this marvelous creation in which we move and have our being. We must find theological language to kindle enthusiasm for our role in the evolutionary process. We must move beyond the desperate, somewhat dismal eschatological literalism of Daniel and Revelation into an eschatology of hope based on our vision of the immediate immanence of God which is forever creating and sustaining the world and the enterprises of justice, mercy, and good faith. God is not dead, even though the God who was a man, a woman, the all-powerful, or "wholly other" has become unwell in our minds and hearts.

Clearly, there is much theological work to be done in bringing our ways of thinking about God into line with what we "know that we know" about our world. We have to go with what we have, but that does not mean we will never have any more. Theology must be forever open to change as new knowledge becomes convincing to our minds.

But the immediate immanence of God must be reckoned with. The fact that we must learn how to abide by the rules that are necessary for our continued existence is not about to change or be suspended. The rules become our whole ecological ethic. The necessity of our obedience to these rules is rooted in our ways of thinking about God. When we gain a full vision of the immediate immanence of God living and acting in the universe which is still evolving, we will understand the reckless spilling of oil into the ocean as a physical assault against God. We will understand the substance abuse of chemicals and drugs as an attack on God's presence. Our perception of vast slums and human beings entrapped to live less than an animal existence will be immediately a horrified consciousness that God is homeless, hungry, filthy, toothless, and doomed to die a derelict's death.

When mainstream Protestants come to our full flower in knowing God as the actor in the events of our world, we will not turn to psychologized religion for escape. We will turn to fresh obedience to the highest whole ecological ethic that we can conceive. This obedience will become our Holy Communion with God who is immediately immanent, closer than heartbeat or breathing. Then we will be able to move forward to what each of us craves deeply in our own way: we will be able to experience epiphany, that glorious emotional and intellectual pleasure that comes when belief has been born into faith in God.

CHAPTER
VIII

OUR HUNGER FOR EPIPHANY

The universal practice of religion suggests that human beings have a natural, a genetic, need for intellectual and emotional communion with the powers that give and sustain life. There are many names for God, but the experience of feeling in some kind of union or harmony with God is yearned for and sought by all human beings. Even when a few persons may seem to have displaced their yearning for God, it is usually apparent that they have put something else into that special position calling for one's dedication and devotion.

I am calling the successful quest for union with God the experience of epiphany. This is a dictionary use of the term. It is also used to designate a special day in the church year. But the experience of epiphany is that genuine sense of knowing and feeling that one's life is, in some degree, in harmony with God, whose mystery transcends our capacities to know in full who or what God is in the divine whole.

Most of us have known fleeting moments, or even longer periods, when all of the difficulties and pleasures of life were diminished by what seemed to be an intruding presence. Wordsworth spoke of this in "Lines Composed a Few Miles Above Tintern Abbey":

> And I have felt
> A presence that disturbs me with the joy
> Of elevated thoughts.

Our hymnals are rich with expressions of profound gratitude that God "is an ever present help in trouble." The psalms reflect a long history of human experience crying out for God and finding answers that do not allow us to doubt that people experienced something valid and lasting in its sustaining powers.

The experience of epiphany may not be harder for us to achieve than it was for our ancestors. We are confronting a universe described by the sciences, and we have our problems with the faceless abyss of space. But our ancestors had harsh circumstances and dangers that most of us do not have to endure. Perhaps we do well to recognize that the experience of epiphany has never been easily achieved. Our need for the experience in our time is urgent if we are to evolve and sustain a whole ecological ethic that will save the human race from self-destruction. Our question is how to achieve the experience of knowing ourselves to be blessed.

The most treacherous ground in religion is on this point, for it is very difficult to distinguish between emotional excess and what may be valid experience of God. Every religious tradition has its problems with this peculiar tendency to identify extravagant emotional experience of one kind or another with what might be a valid experience of the divine that is beyond ordinary intellectual reach.

This is not the place, nor do I have the competence, to solve this problem. But it must be recognized here. What I am willing to say with some certainty is that we do well when we measure our emotional experiences of God with our obedience to an ethic that calls us to a more noble existence.

For good reasons I have been emphasizing beliefs and a whole ecological ethic. Now we must take another step, and it must be taken with great caution.

BELIEF AND FAITH

A church organization cannot live on beliefs alone. When the belief system is convincing and the people have gained a mutual confidence in their shared beliefs, the people can act upon the basis of what they believe. When they do this in the church, their beliefs are transformed or converted into faith, and faith is the stuff out of which epiphany is composed.

Faith is so closely related to trust that I must confess great difficulty in distinguishing between them. I will continue to use the term *faith* here, but I could just as easily speak of trust. I do not mean by either word some kind of blind belief in something that cannot be proved. I have known many people who use *faith* to talk about the things that they believe in spite of having no basis at all for believing what they claim to believe.

When belief is solid enough for us to have faith in the belief, we will be ready to act on the basis of that belief. It is when we have acted on the basis of belief that we achieve faith, and then our hunger for epiphany may be fed by the Bread of Heaven. We are fed with the experience of epiphany when we know that our living is significant because we have lived significantly. How easy to say; how hard to believe and do.

The question of difference between belief and faith was clarified for me by a story that has its roots in my boyhood. I grew up in Las Animas, Colorado. It is an attractive little town which has not changed much through the years. It is situated in an irrigated valley with the Arkansas River on one side of town and the Purgatory River on the other side. Melons, orchards, hay fields, and great cottonwood trees grace the valley.

Kit Carson, Bent's Fort, and Indian writings on canyon walls nearby are historical features. Almost every summer of my boyhood, Las Animas would get set for a visiting street carnival which broke up the long, hot summer. It was an annual affair, and I finally became old enough to be allowed to go alone to watch the carnival workers set things up. The carnival tents and wagons had the smell of distant places. Tattooed pitchmen worked the small crowds even before the sideshow tents were up, and a man did card tricks to help sell bottled tonics and wooden combs that were painted black.

The first year that I was allowed to go alone to see the sights, there was a new attraction. A tightrope walker was scheduled to do a free performance twice a day. On either side of Main Street there were (and still are) three-story buildings built of strong stones. When I arrived on the scene, he had already fastened his wire cable on one of the buildings, and a few people were on the roof of the store across the street where he would fasten the other end. One store belonged to my Uncle Cliff, whose hardware store was open territory for me anytime I chose.

After scrambling up the three flights of stairs leading to the flat roof, I erupted breathlessly onto the roof just in time to hear some men asking what the tightrope performer intended to do. He patiently explained that he would do stunts on the trapeze. He would also walk across the wire without the balancing bar, holding the big, red umbrella. He would do other things.

He didn't make any reference to a fancy wheelbarrow nearby. Its wheel lacked a tire but was grooved to fit the wire. When asked about the wheelbarrow he said, "Oh, I will be blindfolded. Then I will put somebody in it and wheel him across to the other side." There were murmurs of doubt as one person after another said that nobody could do that—all except my Uncle Cliff, who didn't talk much. He remained silent, so one of the men asked him directly, "What do you say, Cliff, can he do it?" My Uncle Cliff answered without blinking an eye, "I believe he can do it." The tightrope artist quickly said to my trusting Uncle Cliff, "Okay, I'll wheel you across."

The story ends there, and I cannot report what my Uncle Cliff did. It just happens to be a powerful illustration that is fictitious. Las Animas is real, and I did grow up there. My Uncle Cliff is still very real to me even now, for he was a gentle Scotsman whom I admired. We did have street carnivals every year, and I recall one that had a tight-rope walker. I did go out on the roof to watch him put the gear into place. He did as the posters had announced—he wheeled somebody across the wire. He didn't ask me to be that person. I am sure that I would have declined. But someone did believe enough to trust the tightrope artist. Whomever that person was, he or she arrived on the other side of the street with the experience of faith displacing abstract belief.

Our experiences of epiphany are something like that. They come to us when we have walked, as Kierkegaard suggested, "in fear and trembling," to do or to act as we believe. In its larger frame, the experience of epiphany is achieved when we have followed our highest visions for human life and the nurture of our earth, our home. When our worship is a celebration of what we have done and what we will commit ourselves to do in healing life and nurturing life, epiphany is almost certain to be experienced from time to time.

BREAKDOWN OF FAITH

In the past, our mainstream Protestant churches derived energy from beliefs strongly endorsed in worship and regularly expressed in compassionate projects at home and abroad. The signal of mainstream Protestant decline was fully seen when the church membership could not see any connection between their beliefs and the new summons to social actions that were political and economic rather than strictly compassionate.

Mainstream Protestants understood compassion expressed in children's homes or hospitals, but challenging the social order seemed to have very little to do with Jesus or with God. Calling for social changes was "getting into politics," and mainstream Christians had no theology for such things. Our beliefs could become faith by giving money to an orphanage, but not by marching in a demonstration against racism on behalf of civil rights. Mainstream Protestants could connect God with compassion for distant heathens or poor people who were invisible. Our theology did not enable us to experience epiphany by acting to challenge social practices that inflicted cruelty on people that we could see. The needy people that we could see were not the kind we played golf with or invited to dinner. Our theology had not brought us into believing that the unlovely woman or man across town is our brother or sister to be loved and served. There was no epiphany for us in the slums in our town, our countryside, or our city.

An illustration of this may help us to understand this problem more vividly. In the mid-1960s, when the churches were really involved in the "War on Poverty," I was interviewed on a television program in a northern state. The interviewer knew how well the churches of his city were supporting a major civil rights project in the South, and he asked me if I admired their dedication. These churches were generous supporters of this particular project in which I was administratively involved rather deeply. I told him that I did admire the generosity and knew how much good it was doing. But I confessed that I had a problem. He invited me to tell about my problem, and this is approximately what I said on the air:

The people of this region are very generous in their support of that project down South. But they don't support a similar project right here in this very city. But the people down South are giving generously to the project in this city. My problem is this: Why can't people support mission projects in their own neighborhoods?

On the day of that broadcast, I really did not know how widely this characterized church behavior all across the nation. Everybody seemed to be ready to do the necessary things to change the social conditions in other lands or distant places, but they did not want to do things like that closer to home. Why not? Now I know. Their beliefs about their role as followers of the Christian way did not include working to achieve changes in the social and economic practices that served them so well. The belief systems in our churches did not unfold before their minds and hearts a vision of God who is working in the evolutionary process today to achieve people who use their intelligence and freedom to create and sustain the connections of mutual support in their own hometown!

They sought escape from risks of local action to achieve change. As a result, they could not enjoy through their group worship an occasional experience of epiphany growing out of their sure knowledge that they had served the living God whose striving in this world today and tomorrow is for the kingdom of love, sharing, and mutuality. Instead of getting into the wheelbarrow and running the risks of a high venture, they hired somebody far away to do it for them. The station got a bushel basket full of mail protesting my statement. Some of the mail implied that I was a man bent on doing some wicked damage to the reputation of the whole region. The reaction was strong enough to force me to be more sympathetic with the church members who felt wounded by my statement, but I was honestly stating my own problem! If what I described were true, was it their fault or was it the fault of church leaders?

EXPERIENCE OF EPIPHANY

Where could I go for an answer to the problem of why people do not achieve the experience of epiphany by doing ordinary things close at hand which express their highest purposes in life? As is so often the case, the answer was in what some people had been telling me all along. In my own case, my question had been answered long ago, but I had not yet heard the answer.

When I was in college, long before I made a final decision to be a pastor, I shared in running a storefront mission in Nicholasville, Kentucky. It was my task to conduct Sunday afternoon services. I worked in the college bakery and had to go to work every morning at four o'clock. Sunday was a day that I looked forward to for some extra sleep, and the Sunday afternoon service was a chore that I sometimes dreaded. My classmate who had started the mission had told me about one woman who was our major supporter through her gift of a little less than one dollar per week.

She had several children and took in washing for a living. There was no welfare or support of any kind at that time. She was on her own all the way. One day I asked her about the large amount she was giving and implied that it might be reduced by a dime a week. She looked at me with a radiant face and said, "Giving that money is the best thing I do." I believe she experienced epiphany when we sang hymns, joined in prayer, and groped for God's presence in our lives. Her beliefs connected her life to great purposes because in that storefront mission she saw their realization.

Many years later, a widow who had confided to me the details of her finances made a sizeable pledge to a special project in our church. I felt that I had been given a certain responsibility to butt into her affairs, so I visited her at home and asked her if she hadn't gone overboard a bit. She was not offended in the least. She thanked me and said, "This is the only thing that makes me feel life is worth living." I was chastened, but I am not sorry that I called on her. She reminded me that I had forgotten a valuable lesson taught by the woman in the Nicholasville mission.

Every pastor has many experiences of a similar kind. My point is not the stories but my failure to understand that these people, and all the rest of us, achieve the experience of epiphany in doing ordinary things that are extensions of our deeply felt beliefs. That woman who took in washing in Nicholasville and the widow who gave what seemed like an overly large pledge are typical human beings acting on the basis of beliefs that became faith through their acting in a risky venture (giving money was a risk for them!). The culminating experience was radiance, a sense of meaning, and union with God—epiphany.

We have begun to formulate an ethic for the twenty-first century, and everywhere we look we see with our own eyes that this must go beyond a social ethic to become a whole ecological ethic. We moved faster with our ethical development than we did with our theology and biblical understanding. We found ourselves unable to achieve epiphany because our services of worship, our prayers, our exhortations were all out of touch with the modern world. The malnourishment of our belief systems made it impossible for us to get into the wheelbarrow and risk our lives by crossing to the other side where we would know the inner thrill of being more than we thought we were. We who are assigned leadership roles are paralyzed.

Our task in mainstream Protestantism is not to indulge in the contrivance of tricks to excite the emotional side of personality. We had enough of that in the revival period. It would be a false move to begin to measure our recovery from paralysis in leadership to rate success in terms of the ability of leaders to plan and execute big rallies where there is a lot of emotional display. The experience of epiphany is the achievement of faith through experience in validating our beliefs in ethical actions.

We must learn how to speak of God as immediately

immanent in the ecological crisis as well as actively alive in our personal ethical struggles. We must feel ourselves to be an extension of the biblical saga: we, the new women and men of a new age born out of our freedom and intelligence, made to be useful creators with God. We must have more faithful, painstaking preparation of liturgies, hymns, prayers, and exhortations that celebrate evolving beliefs and growing ethics. We must choose specific avenues of action that are directly linked to our beliefs and ethic. Then when the beliefs, the ethic, the action, and the worship come together, each reinforcing the other, we experience our union with God—epiphany.

We American mainstream Protestants have given much to our nation and to the world. We have passed through our first great era of vitality and now must be radically converted for the new era that is already enveloping all of us. The need is great.

We will not be able to address the new opportunities of the years ahead unless we break up our stolid resistance to the new theological and biblical knowledge that calls for us to rid our language of the fundamentalist jargon. We will learn to speak in new metaphors. Mainstream Protestantism waits for a new birth in its leadership. Only through intensive hermeneutic conversations that open us up in our doubts can we expand the range of our affirmations. It is time to abandon old wineskins. There is a new theological and biblical wine that is waiting, and we should not neglect it.

I look forward to new experiences of epiphany in the years ahead as we suffer and flounder our way to a recovery from our malnourished condition. The ways of hermeneutic conversation are the ways of Pentecost, and flames resting upon our shoulders may sometimes seem too near for comfort. But epiphany is worth it.

ENDNOTES

1. THE MAINSTREAM PROTESTANTS AT BAY

1. Constant H. Jaquet, ed., *Yearbook of American and Canadian Churches* (Abingdon Press, 1989). *The Yearbook of the American and Canadian Churches* is updated every year by the National Council of Churches in the United States of America. I draw these statistics from the 1989 issue and am rounding off the figures for the sake of ease in getting a fair picture.

2. G. M. Marsden, *Fundamentalism and American Culture: The Shaping of Twentieth-Century Evangelicalism*, 1870-1925 (Oxford University Press, 1980).

3. Ibid.

4. Don Cupitt, *The Sea of Faith* (Cambridge University Press, 1988).

5. Laurence Shames, *The Hunger for More: Searching for Values in the Age of Greed* (Times Books, 1989). My reference is dependent on an excerpt in the *New York Times,* 4 Dec. 1988, *Business World* supplement, p. 30.

6. Quoted in the *New York Times,* 18 Dec. 1988.

7. *New York Times,* 18 Dec. 1988.

8. I developed this thesis on the basis of data from Oscar Ornati of the New School for Social Research in New York. My book was titled *Keepers of the Poor* (Mission Press, 1966, now out of print).

9. Benjamin DeMott, "Rediscovering Complexity," *The Atlantic,* September 1988.

10. Rodney Stark and Charles Y. Glock, *American Piety: The Nature of Religious Commitment* (The University of California Press, 1968), p. 217.

11. Dean Kelley, *Why the Conservative Churches Are Growing* (Harper & Row, 1966).

12. W. H. Auden, *The Collected Poetry of W. H. Auden* (Random House, 1945), pp. 428-29.

13. Ibid.

2. PSYCHOLOGIZING RELIGION

1. Don S. Browning, *Religious Thought and the Modern Psychologies: A Critical Conversation in the Theology of Culture* (Fortress Press: 1987).

2. Norman Vincent Peale, *The True Joy of Positive Living* (William Morrow & Co., 1984).

3. Ibid.

4. *Studies in Third World Societies, Part I: Missionaries, Anthropologists, and Cultural Change; Part II: Missionaries and Anthropologists,* The Department of Anthropology, College of William and Mary, Williamsburg, VA 23185. (It might be helpful to read Part II first.)

5. Peter McKenzie, *The Christians: Their Practices and Beliefs* (Abingdon Press, 1988; co-published in Britain: SPCK, 1988).

6. William Henry Bernhardt, *The Cognitive Quest for God and Operational Theism* (The Criterion Press, 1971), p. 192.

3. THE MALNOURISHED CHURCH

1. Daniel Katz and Robert L. Kahn, *The Social Psychology of Organizations* (John Wiley and Sons, 1966), pp. 52-53.

2. Alfred, Lord Tennyson, *In Memoriam,* part 46, stanza 3.

3. John W. de Gruchy, *Theology and Ministry in Context and Crisis* (William B. Eerdmans, 1987), p. 46.

4. Byron L. Rohrig, "No Clergy Shortage by 2001." *Circuit Rider* 13, no. 6 (July/August 1989), p. 8.

4. THE PARALYSIS OF MAINSTREAM LEADERSHIP

1. Kenneth E. Boulding, *The Image* (The University of Michigan Press, 1956). The first three chapters of this book are not excelled in their discussion of the image as a nurturing element in organizations. This study has weathered the tests of time.

2. Edward Farley, *The Fragility of Knowledge: Theological Education in the Church and University* (Fortress, 1988).

3. L. Gregory Jones, *Toward a Recovery of Theological Discourse in United Methodism, Quarterly Review* 9, no. 2 (Summer 1989), p. 25.

5. HEALING THE WOUND OF OUR DIVISION

1. Robert Wuthnow, *The Restructuring of American Religion: Society and Faith Since World War II* (Princeton University Press, 1988), p. 134.
2. George Lindbeck, *"Scripture, Consensus, and Community,"* This *World* no. 23 (Fall 1988), p. 21.
3. Edgar V. McKnight, *Post-Modern Use of the Bible: The Emergence of Reader-Oriented Criticism* (Abingdon Press, 1988), p. 217 ff.
4. William F. Fore, *Television and Religion: The Shaping of Faith, Values, and Culture* (Augsburg Publishing House, 1987). A splendid adaptation of this book's central theme was printed in the *Quarterly Review* (Winter 1988).

6. THE RECOVERY OF JESUS

1. Robert W. Funk, Bernard Brandon Scott, and James R. Butts, *The Parables of Jesus: Red Letter Edition* (Polebridge Press, 1988), p. 3.
2. Brevard S. Childs, *The New Testament as Canon: An Introduction* (Fortress Press, 1984).
3. Amos N. Wilder, *Jesus' Parables and the War of Myths: Essays on Imagination in the Scriptures* (Fortress Press, 1982).
4. Norman Perrin, *Jesus and the Language of the Kingdom: Symbol and Metaphor in New Testament Interpretation* (Fortress Press, 1976).
5. Norman Perrin, *Recovering the Teachings of Jesus* (Fortress Press, 1976).

7. THE IMMEDIATE IMMANENCE OF GOD AND A WHOLE ECOLOGICAL ETHIC

1. Sallie McFague, *Models of God: A Theology for an Ecological, Nuclear Age* (Fortress Press, 1987), part II: pp. 91-180.
2. James Moulder, "Why Feminist Theology Encourages Unbelief," in *Paradigms and Progress in Theology*. 1988. Human Sciences Research Council, Praetoria 0001, South Africa. pp. 252-58.
3. Ian Barbour, *Myths, Models, and Paradigms: A Comparative Study In Science* (Harper & Row, 1974). Also, *Science and Secularity: The Ethics of Technology* (Harper & Row, 1970), pp. 18-22.